ISBN 978-1-331-12819-9
PIBN 10033835

1 MONTH OF
FREE
READING

at
www.ForgottenBooks.com

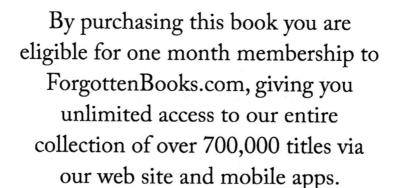

By purchasing this book you are eligible for one month membership to ForgottenBooks.com, giving you unlimited access to our entire collection of over 700,000 titles via our web site and mobile apps.

To claim your free month visit:

www.forgottenbooks.com/free33835

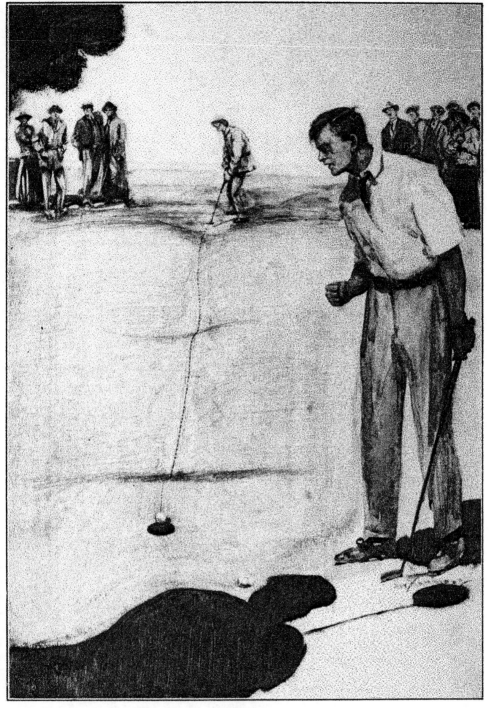

"THE MOST WONDERFUL PUTT (ONE BY TRAVIS) IT HAS EVER BEEN
MY LOT TO WITNESS"

" It took the slope to the right, wound its way along this raised mound and, winding, turning, twisting up-slope and down-slope, it broke in at exactly the
right spot, and then it plumped squarely into the center of the cup"

THE WINNING SHOT

BY

JEROME D. TRAVERS

*Open Champion and Four Times Amateur Golf
Champion of the United States*

AND

GRANTLAND RICE

Illustrated

GARDEN CITY   NEW YORK
DOUBLEDAY, PAGE & COMPANY
1916

DEDICATED TO THE DUFFER

This is the substance of our Plot—
For those who play the Perfect Shot,
There are ten thousand who do not.

For each who comes to growl and whine
Because one putt broke out of line
And left him but a Sixty-Nine,

At least ten thousand on the slate
Rise up and cheer their blessed fate
Because they got a Ninety-Eight.

For each of those who rarely sees,
Amid his run of Fours and Threes,
A Trap or Bunker—if you please—

Ten thousand Blighted Souls are found
Who daily pummel, pierce, or pound
The scourging sand-heaps underground.

DEDICATED TO THE DUFFER

Who is it pays the major fee
For rolling green and grassy tee?
Who is it, Reader?—answer me!

The scattered few in countless clubs
Who sink their putts as if in tubs,
Or eke the half a million dubs?

He may not have the Taylor Flip—
He may not know the Vardon Grip—
He may not Pivot at the Hip—

And we will say his Follow Through
Is frequently somewhat askew,
Or halting, as if clogged with Glue—

Yet, Splashers in the Wayside Brook,
To you who foozle, slice, and hook,
We dedicate This Little Book.

Not that your Style enthralls the eye
But that there are, to spring the Why,
So many more of you to Buy.

PREFACE

There has been an abundance of golf literature which deals in the technical method of playing each shot.

But there is a great deal more to golf than any mere mechanism of form. There is also a wonderful psychology, an elastic humour, the thrill of many mighty matches and miraculous shots that add greatly to its lure.

There are also many inside tips and various suggestions a trifle off the beaten path that may furnish more real aid to improvement in play than any detailed accounts of grip and stance and swing.

Too often the essential things for improvement in play are overlooked in following a certain routine that may suit one where it is utterly unfit for another.

So the object of this book is not to present any definite instruction along established lines, but to take a wider scope: to range out into golf psychology—to show the value of concentration and control of nerves—and to entertain, if possible, with stories of championship matches and champion players; to show how these matches were won with certain shots or by unusual temperaments.

It has been the good fortune of one of the co-authors to have played against or to have seen the best golfers in Great Britain and America; which has made it possible to get first-hand information of how the Hiltons, Balls, Vardons, Travises, Ouimets, and Evanses go about their work of beating Par and reducing Bogie to subjection; to show what the game's greatest stars have done, and along broader lines, about how they do it— their strength and their weaknesses—with the entire scheme of things surrounded with incident and anecdote and opinion that help to illustrate the situation.

The idea is to both instruct and entertain—to follow the way of the Ancient Green in its devious windings, and turn the spotlight on those things that should appeal to the golfer's fancy—not only of the low-handicap man, but of the duffer as well—as long as he has caught the *spirit of the game or has felt, even in slight measure, its insistent appeal. Those playing golf in America are now verging upon the million, including all varieties of life and existence, and to these "The Winning Shot" is offered in the hope that it may help to increase the lure of the Nineteenth Hole.*

THE AUTHORS.

CONTENTS

ILLUSTRATIONS

AYE, MACPHEARSON?

("Golf has become too easy."—Mr. Herbert Fowler.)

"Golf has become too easy?"   Aye, MacPhearson,
   We know, we know with ninety-sixes net,
Who first get bad and later on get worse'n
   We ever dreamed a half-blind rat could get;
Who top our drive into some ghastly grotto
   Or plump a mashie where some trap lies hid,
Who down the green know but one dismal motto:
      "Slip me a niblick, kid."

"Golf has become too easy?"   Aye, aye, Sandy—
   We ken, we ken who swat one from the tee
And shoot our trusty iron for a dandy,
   Some seven paces from a perfect "three."
And then we grab our likewise trusty putter
   And putt and putt and putt around the cup
Until we find, as we profanely mutter:
      "The other guy's 'six up.'"

AYE, MACPHEARSON?

"Golf has become too easy?" Oh! you Fowler—
  O rarest optimist of all the breed;
No need for you to rush the cheering growler,
  Or lamp this page for any uplift screed;
If some uncanny fate, its purpose wreaking,
  Should some day drop you to the burning wold,
Our ears shall be attuned to hear you shrieking:
    "Hell has become too cold!"

THE WINNING SHOT

THE average golfer starts out upon his round of the course with an average of seven clubs, which are likely to be driver, brassie, cleek, mid-iron, mashie, niblick, and putter.

If each one of these clubs was of equal value in the task of securing the proper score, upon the basis of 100 per cent. for the round, each club would represent a playing usefulness of about 14 per cent. But this is where the system cracks. There is one club in the bag that has a greater value than 14 per cent. It is the shortest, lightest, and smallest club of the entire lot, the simplest and yet the hardest to play, the club that many unknowns can handle well and yet a club that baffles an Evans and a Vardon from one year into another. I refer to the putter, and I put its playing value at 45 per cent. as against 55 per cent. for the remaining six, seven, or eight clubs needed for the round.

"Forty-five per cent. is too high a rating for any one club," a number of experts have said to me; but if I have made a mistake here it is on the short side. I only wish some of those who underrate the tremendous value of the putter had been at Brookline when the Open Championship of America was at stake. If they had, they would have gone well beyond my computation and put the value of the putter at 75 per cent. Alec Smith, the well-known professional, kept track of different scores turned in through this tournament, and he figures that of every one hundred shots played, seventy-five were taken on the putting green. It was no uncommon sight there to see crack golfers reach greens over four hundred yards away in two perfectly played shots, and then scatter three or four putts all over the green before the bottom of the cup was reached. I saw one crack professional get

[4]

within four feet of a four-hundred-yard hole in two shots and finally get down in six. He missed his three, went well below the cup, and then took three more coming back. And he was no exception to the rule.

THE CASE OF CHICK EVANS

Undoubtedly "the winning shot" in golf is the putt. There can be no question about it. Take the case of Charles Evans, Jr., of Chicago, and myself. Our game, our different styles of play, have been compared from one end of the country to the other for the past three or four years. But the Fates were kinder to me than they were to Evans. They gave Evans a perfect driving style from the tee and almost always sure results. They gave him control of the mid-iron and the mashie, where in my opinion he is unexcelled by any amateur I have ever seen. They took him in triumph from the tee up to the green—a perfect golfing machine—and then, right at the finish, they denied him the simplest, yet often the hardest, shot in the bag—the putt.

On the other hand, the Fates have often led me in a roundabout way before I came within sight of the green. My weakness has been with the wood, the club that counts less in general value. But I have been strongest where Evans has been weakest, and the comparative values of driving and putting can be shown in the statement that I have won four Amateur Championships, while the very fine young Chicago golfer has yet to win his first. In match play he had every shot except one—and that happened to be "the winning shot" of golf—the shot that makes up for a bad drive, a poor mashie pitch, or a poor approach, by calling for but one putt to the green at the moment of need.

SOME WONDER WORK

During the last championship at Garden City I watched Evans practising one morning. I watched with some envy the very fine way he drove a dozen perfectly hit balls from the tee, straight down the course. Then I saw him station his caddie one hundred and fifty yards away, and play twenty-five iron shots in succession within six feet of where that boy stood. Shot after shot left the club on a perfect line and at perfect height, dropping within easy reach of the caddie's hand. There wasn't another golfer in the tournament who could have approached this work. It was almost miraculous.

And then, a few minutes later on, I saw him putting, and I knew then that he still had a lot of trouble ahead of him, for even in practice it was easy to see that this one shot was still denied him. He lacked the confident bearing, and the easy, pendulum swing with the right follow through had not yet come. And yet, before any one blames Evans for this, it should be remembered that the same fault belongs to Harry Vardon, the great English professional, who in other respects is far and away the grandest golfer of all time. If Vardon's putting was up to the rest of his game, he could give any golfer alive four strokes and romp home in front. If Evans could putt like Walter J. Travis it would be foolish to stage an Amateur

Championship in this country. The result would be written down in advance.

OUIMET'S PUTTING

Francis Ouimet, America's young Open Champion, did very fine work at Brookline with wood and iron. But with these he was certainly no better than Vardon and Ray. He was not so good. But he achieved a feat beyond all other record incidents, and sent his name spinning on through golfing history because, when the time came, he could thump the ball into the cup from almost any angle or distance on the green. He was putting like a champion, and all the wizard work of Vardon and Ray up to the greens couldn't offset the young American's ability within twenty feet of the cup, where he was either "in" or "dead" to the hole on his next shot.

I consider this no fluke, because I know that Ouimet is a very fine putter, and one with a wonderful temperament for the game. He has a beautiful putting stroke, stands well over the ball, and with the necessary pendulum motion has a perfect follow through. If you follow his play you will rarely find him short on any putt. He always gives the ball a chance, and at Brookline last fall he also gave several thousand a series of nervous shocks by the way in which he ran on three and four feet past the cup— whenever he missed. But he always holed coming back, showing that his confidence was supreme.

HARD FIGHT AHEAD

When I met Ouimet for the first time at Garden City in the 1913 championship, I had not formed any opinion as to the work I had ahead until I saw him make his first putt. Then I knew that I had my work cut out, for this part of his game impressed me at once, and I knew what it meant to meet a high-class putter in match play. He soon began dropping eight-, ten-, and twelve-footers, and I had all I could do to stay with him. In fact, at the end of twenty-five holes I was one down with a good chance of losing the twenty-sixth, until I managed to stick a long iron shot up and go down in one putt.

NEW ANGLE

There is a new angle in this connection that I should like to bring out. We all know that there is less of the physical and more of the psychological in putting than in any other part of golf. To be putting well the golfer must have absolute control of his nerves, for nervousness shows more upon the green than anywhere else. If a drive is ten feet off line no great damage results, as a rule, but if a putt is one half of an inch off line the shot is absolutely wasted. So it is my belief that a man must conserve his nervous force if he is to keep putting well through a tournament.

You may get an example of this by watching Mathewson pitch a ball game. He works just about hard enough to win. If the Giants give Mathewson five or six runs to work on, you never see him trying to pitch his arm off for a shut-out. He is content to take it fairly easy, always keeping his game well in hand, but never working at top speed until they begin to crowd him again. In this way he can keep in better shape for emergencies, and his arm won't feel the bad effects at his next start.

It's the same way in golf. I know how hard it is, what a strain there is attached, in winning an Amateur Championship at match play. For this reason I pay no attention to the medal-play round except to try and qualify safely. I merely take it as it comes, not bothering over any missed shots, because I am not looking for any medal-score victories. If my first match is fairly easy I drift quietly along with it, and feel quite content to win by a fairly small margin. Then when the actual test comes later on in the week, I am still fresh and well able to meet it at top form.

I have kept track of all the amateur championships of the United States, and with two exceptions I have yet to see the winner of the medal round come through and win the championship. These two exceptions were Harold Hilton at Apawamis, in 1911, and Walter J. Travis many years ago. Hilton won the low medal score and also the championship at match play. But I can recall no other who has been able to do both. Evans has won, as I recall it, five of the last seven medal-play rounds. But this has worked against him in championship match play.

It is hard in any game for a man to start off at top speed and hold the pace to the end. When a golfer wins a medal-play round he has set a fast pace from the jump, has already started the drain upon his nervous system, and later on in the week, after successive grinds of thirty-six-hole matches, this pace will begin to tell. And where this nervous strain will show most is likely to be in putting. When a man begins to break under the drive and the wear and tear of match play, it is generally the putter that starts to tell the story. And for this reason I don't believe in a golfer starting out to win or try and win a medal-play round when his main goal is still six days away, six days of heartbreaking, nerve-racking play, with many moments ahead where he will need all the reserve force at his command to control a situation.

THE ART OF PUTTING

"I know well enough," remarked a golfer recently, "that putting is the most valuable part of golf. But how can a poor putter learn to become a good one?"

The answer is obvious: By practising, and practising only in the right way. You see golfers standing on a tee practising driving for an hour or so at a time, or putting the same time into iron shots. And then perhaps they will practise putting ten or fifteen minutes. When I started golf I spent as much time, or more, at putting as I did with all other clubs put together. I worked for hours at a time—worked, worked, and worked until I obtained confidence in my club. I have frequently practised putting all the morning, and then have gone out to play in the afternoon, when I had the day off for play.

But at the same time one must practise intelligently. Routine practice without giving any thought to the shot will not help nearly so much.

To become a good putter I believe that a man should stand well over the ball, so that he can all the easier get the line of the putt. I don't believe in stooping over too far, for this is likely to develop a feeling of cramped play. And by standing fairly erect there isn't the same tendency to jab or stab at the ball as there is when one is crouched with the putter held low. The good putter should swing the club with a pendulum motion, using his hands and wrists with the body perfectly still. And by all means he should look at the ball and *not* the hole, despite advice given to the contrary. If all golfers would practise looking at the ball, looking at the back of it, just where the club should strike, they would soon find an immediate improvement in this part of their game. But most of them, when they do practise, forget about this important feature. Try this scheme of looking at the ball until the putter has started it upon the way to the hole, and you will be surprised at the number of strokes you can save in a single round.

The point I am trying to bring out is that the putt is the winning shot in golf, the one shot to be developed above all others. I don't mean to say that driving and iron play are not important. They are, of course. But no other two clubs in the bag, combined, are as important as the putter, in so far as the art of scoring is concerned.

"COULDN'T MISS A PUTT"

Two men come back together toward the clubhouse from a round at tournament golf.

Get the loser off to one side and ask him just how he managed to get beaten. Nine times out of ten he won't even refer to his opponent's good driving or his iron play. "Why," he'll say, "the fellow couldn't miss a putt. He was holding the ball from any old distance or angle. I never had a chance."

Or, more than likely, he will hand you this: "I was playing well enough except that my putting was off.

I took three putts on four greens, and missed three or four easy ones I should have landed. Why, if I had been putting even fairly well——" etc., etc.

It's always the putter that comes in for most of the post-mortem conversation. If a man is putting well he is a hard man for any one to beat. If he is putting poorly there isn't much chance for him to win.

VARDON VS. McDERMOTT

Take the case of Vardon against McDermott, conceded by most to be the greatest all-round golfers in England and America respectively. They met twice in America in the same competitions. The first time was at Shawnee. In that first meeting they were about the same from the tee and through the fairway up to the putting green. But McDermott was putting steadily, taking two putts to the green only and getting most of his four-footers. Vardon's putting, on the other hand, was quite erratic. He was uncertain upon three- and four-foot putts and uncertain as to getting down in two from fifteen or twenty feet away. The result was that McDermott, at the end of seventy-two holes, led the wonderful English player by thirteen or fourteen strokes—an exceptionally wide margin and all picked up in apparently the simplest part of the game.

In any professional tournament it is always the one who is putting that wins the money. There is no great difference among the leaders from the tee or in their iron play. But on the day of the tournament two or three from the bunch will fall into a fine putting streak, and they will be unbeatable. And if they are not putting exceptionally well they stand very little chance.

To continue the case of Vardon and McDermott: McDermott was playing very good golf at Brookline in the last American Open Championship, about as well as he had played at Shawnee the month before. But a certain unfortunate incident had arisen in connection with a remark McDermott is said to have made regarding the two British golfers, and the American came in for a certain amount of criticism. The incident was enough to get decidedly upon his nerves, and the result immediately showed in his putting. This part of his game fell away, a part of his wonderful confidence vanished—for there never was a more confident golfer in any tournament—and McDermott's putting suffered far beyond any other part of his game. So in place of leading Vardon thirteen or fourteen strokes, it was Vardon who led the chief American hope by a fair margin. And Vardon was headed off in turn, not by any seasoned professional who was master of wood and iron, but by a twenty-year-old amateur who knew the shortest distance on the green from the ball into the centre of the cup.

CONTROL OF EMOTIONS

One of the main points attached to good putting is control over emotions. The golfer who misses a putt and then immediately goes into the air has a hard time ahead. He must develop the habit of forgetting a bad shot and centering his entire atten-

[18]

tion upon the next hole on beyond. Many a fine golfer who had a good chance to win some important tournament has lost out because he let a bad putt get upon his nerves.

To show the importance of developing this temperament, take the case of Alec Smith. Three or four years ago Smith came to the last hole with a chance to win the Open Championship of America. At the last green it had settled to one short putt, a putt of less than three feet. He had that putt left to become champion. He stepped up, putted, and missed. It must have been a hard blow to him, but if he was upset no one in the crowd could tell it from his expression. He had himself too well under control. And in place of brooding over his misfortune he very promptly forgot about it, and in the playoff from the triple tie which had resulted with himself, J. J. McDermott, and young Macdonald Smith, Alec resumed at his old pace and won handily. The ordinary golfer, after having come that close to victory only to miss an easy shot, would have faded out.

Almost the same thing happened one year in the Metropolitan Open. There was keen rivalry between Alec Smith and Jack McDermott, who have won most of the American Open Championships of late years. They were playing at Salisbury, New Jersey, and the play was nip and tuck. One stroke might decide the match. Coming to a short hole, a par three, Smith pitched to the green. His approach putt ran up within three feet of the hole. He putted for his three and missed, the ball trickling eighteen inches beyond the cup. Then, careless for the moment, he putted loosely for his four and missed that, taking four putts and requiring a five at an acute stage of the match.

This loss of two strokes under such conditions would have unnerved most golfers. Smith was apparently undisturbed. "Oh, I'll get those two back somewhere else," he remarked as he walked to the next tee. He promptly eliminated that disastrous hole from his mental make-up, forgot all about it, stuck to his work as if nothing had happened, and finally won by a small margin. If he had let the loss of those two putts stick with him for even one hole, he probably would have been eliminated. But he had made it a matter of habit to try and forget all the bad turns of fortune, and to play each hole as if he were making a fresh start.

Compare Smith's case with that of thousands who, after missing a putt, show their temper or their worry, and who seem to be unable to forget their latest mistake. A golfer can practise the development of the right mental condition just as he can practise the development of a swing. Too many people make their practice purely physical.

I know in my own case, earlier in my career, I have lost my temper and always with disastrous effects. I lost a good chance to win a championship by getting into a rage because a photographer snapped his camera just as I was playing my shot. I was up at the time in an important match, but went all to pieces and was soon beaten badly. After that experience I made a point of keeping my temper well under control, of accepting each shot and each condition as it came. It was hard work, but I was more than repaid. Only last fall, in the Amateur Championship, when my opponent had just sunk a long putt, a friend of his cheered just as I was starting to try for mine. In earlier years this outbreak, almost at my elbow, would have got on my nerves. But I refused to let it bother me, waited a moment, and then managed to get down a fifteen-footer for a half.

THE SHORT GAME IN GENERAL

Not only putting, but the short game in general, must be cultivated. The chip shot from off the green is a highly important one. When Ouimet was fighting for his chance to tie Vardon and Ray at Brookline, this shot came to his help in wonderful fashion. Coming to the last four holes he had to finish under par with 4-3-3-4 to have a chance. At the fifteenth he played his approach badly, and the ball sailed out to the right of the green, well off line.

FRANCIS OUIMET PUTTING IN HIS MATCH AGAINST VARDON AND RAY

The green was a treacherous one and he had to get fairly close to nail his needed four. If he hadn't had full control of this shot, America's hope would have faded then and there. But he chipped up dead within a foot of the cup and saved the occasion.

THE PSYCHOLOGY OF PUTTING

There is nothing that so jolts an opponent as a long putt that finds the cup. I have had a better chance than most to observe this feature through my own erratic work from the tee. In many a match my opponent has outdriven me, and played a far better second shot. He would be on the green in two, while I was off in the rough in two. Naturally it looked an easy hole for him. But after coming up in three and then sinking a ten or a fifteen putt for a four, the situation had suddenly changed. In place of having the hole without a fight, he suddenly found himself with a three- or a four-foot putt for a half. Two or three holes of this type are enough to get upon any golfer's nerves, however strong they may seem.

I know, because I've had the same medicine handed back to me. And as it is easier to play with your nerves unruffled, I would rather be the one to be getting down the twelve- and fifteen-footers for a four than to be called on to sink the four-foot putts for a half. It works with double force. You are elated and your opponent is correspondingly depressed—if he misses—which he will soon start doing if such conditions as these continue for a hole or two.

THE NEXT SHOT

Next to putting, what is known as the "second shot" is the most valuable in the game. If a man has control of his mid-iron or mashie he is always dangerous. This shot is much more important in my opinion than the tee shot. And in regard to the mashie I have noticed an interesting shift of late. I watched Vardon closely when at work with his club, and saw that he did not take nearly so much turf as most golfers do. In fact, he took very little, playing a much more delicate stroke.

This second shot is the one wherein the professionals as a rule have a big advantage over most amateurs. A first-class amateur is likely to drive as well as a professional, or in close range. He is likely to putt as well. But there are few amateurs who can use mid-iron and mashie with those who make a living from the game. One of the main points to remember in playing this shot is to keep your head still, your eye glued on that ball, and not to sway the body. Most golfers want to do too much work. They are not content to let the club help them out or to figure in the stroke. Arms, body, legs, and head are all used in a wild jumble that brings on disaster. In both putting and approaching more shots are missed by moving the head than through any other agency.

ANOTHER AID

Here is still another aid to the short game in golf, that is, the practice of concentration. Never take your mind off your play for a second. This is a fault, this lack of concentration, that many very fine golfers have. They don't come by it naturally and they have never practised it. If all the best friends I ever had in the world were following a match in which I was playing, I would never know they were around. I have seen Travis in a friendly four-ball match fail even to smile when some one sprung a good joke. He would be so intent upon the play that he would refuse to let any outside element enter his thoughts. And then, later on in the clubhouse, after the match was over, he would probably recall the joke or the funny incident with a laugh.

This matter of concentration is one too often overlooked in golf. It is especially needed around the putting greens, where a perfect coördination of brain and muscle are required, and where the shot is so delicate that the slightest slip means failure. And in golf, if he will, a man can practise thinking, practise with his head as well as with his legs and arms and feet.

In this matter of golfing temperament and concentration Ouimet is far above the average. He has the ideal disposition for a winning player. His mind is centered entirely upon the game from the first shot to the last, and he doesn't get flurried or upset over any bad luck or poor shot. In many ways he is much like Frank Baker of home-run Athletic fame. A championship game to either of these is the same as any other game—all in a day's play. The crowd doesn't get upon their nerves for they don't see the crowd. They forget it is around.

If Evans could develop this temperament and this concentration he would be almost unbeatable. It may come later on. It will undoubtedly be greatly accelerated when he manages to win his first championship.

In going back to the winning shot in golf—that is the putt—there are a few condensed suggestions that in conclusion I would like to give:

1. Stand well over the ball and keep your head still.

2. Keep your eye on that ball and don't move your body.

3.   Cut out the jab or the stab, learn the pendulum swing, and get a follow through with the club.

4.   Cultivate, in practice as well as play, the knack of being a trifle beyond the hole if you miss.   Make a steady practice of giving the ball a chance.

5.   Cultivate the habit of concentration.

6.   Cultivate the habit of confidence and determination, for mental faults can be improved as well as physical ones.

7.   And then practise putting wherever and whenever you get the chance.

SING ON

O sing, Homeric Lyre, the story of my scores;

Sing of the Pars I've cracked—my run of "eighty-
fours";

Sing of the daring shots I've thumped by trap and
ditch,

The story of my drives, my mashie shots, my pitch;

The putts I should have sunk (which wouldn't sink
for me),

But would have, had they dropped, returned a Sixty-
Three;

The mid-iron shots afar, cut with the proper spin,

I swept upon their way six inches from the pin;

Of cleek shots, straight and true, that might have come
from Braid,

Of Brassies through the wind a Vardon might have
made;

Sing, at the Nineteenth Hole, the song of my desire,

The story of my scores, O sing, Homeric Liar.

THE CONUNDRUM OF THE GOLF SHOPS
(Halving It with Colonel Kipling)

When the flush of a newborn sun first fell on Eden's
golfing strand,
Our Father Adam stood on a tee with a crooked stick in
his hand;
And the first rude swing that the world had seen brought
joy to his heart in a swarm,
Till the Devil whispered behind the leaves, "It's pretty—
but is it Form?"

Wherefore he called to his wife and tried to fashion his
swing anew;
The first of the clan who cared a fig for the first great
dread review;

And he left his style to the use of his sons, who thought
    it a glorious gain,
Till the Devil whispered, "Is it Form?" in the ear of
    the duffer Cain.

They builded a bunker to reach the sky and turn each
    score to a blotch;
Till the Devil grunted from out the sand, "It's striking
    —but is it Scotch?"
The cleek was dropped to the bunker side and the idle
    mashie hung,
While each guy talked of the "proper stroke" and each
    in an alien tongue.

When the flicker of springtime's sun first falls with a
    dream that is ever fond,
The sons of Adam hie them forth where the fairway lies
    beyond;
Their brassies sweep as they hit the pill, but their pain
    and their anguish swarm,
For the Devil mutters behind the tee, "You hit it; but
    was it Form?"

II

GETTING BACK ON YOUR GAME

W HEN Jones comes in at night with a desperate look in his eye, and a large grouch with it, barely speaking to his family as he slouches over in a corner out of the way, Mrs. Jones knows the answer.

Five or six years ago she would have been badly upset if she had seen her husband in any such fix. She would have been undecided as to whether he had just failed in business, or had committed murder, or had been poisoned. But having been a "golf widow" for several years, Jones doesn't have to tell her that he "was badly off his game"—slicing, hooking, topping, or something else all the afternoon.

This "off his game ailment" is one of our most prevalent and obnoxious diseases. It claims more victims than any other four scourges known. There are said to be eight hundred thousand people playing golf in the United States now, and of this number it is safe to say that seven hundred and ninety thousand are "badly off their game" over half the time.

This state of affairs results from various causes. In the first place, there is no other game in existence where just a slight deviation from the right way of doing things will result in such damage to the play. In baseball, if the swing is a trifle late, the player may well hit a long double to right field in place of a single to left. But in golf such a swing would almost surely bring the ball up in some deep trap or in other trouble where from one to three shots could be easily lost.

Then again, a golfer who averages around ninety-five for the eighteen holes will some day lose control of himself and shoot an eighty-four. And from that point on "his game"—his regular "game"—is eighty-four, as he hunts in vain for some remedy to bring him back. As this golfer will very probably move back up to ninety-five again, he is always "off his game" from that point on.

If some expert could invent sure remedies for putting each golfer back on his "game," for correcting a slice, a hook, or the many other faults which arise, he could pick up a million dollars a year. He could ask his own price and still get all the customers he could look after, working twenty-four hours a day at his trade. As it is, there are a good many suggestions which, if properly tried, will be of much help, and these are always in order.

EVEN THE BEST GO WRONG

I'll never forget my own harrowing experience at Garden City in the Amateur Championship. I had drawn a rather fortunate spring and summer, and had been going at my best since May in almost every tournament. So when the Amateur Championship came on, I had fair confidence in my ability to make at least a good fight to retain my title.

And then the unexpected happened. It was like

being shot from behind! The day before the tournament started, before the qualifying medal round was to be played, my mashie went wrong. Any man who knows anything about golf knows the importance of this club, the big part it plays in the game. It is a club vital to success, and here, without warning, I was playing it all over the lot. Nearly every shot I hit twisted and spun off at right angles from the correct line. I tried every way I knew to correct the fault, but without success.

The next day the medal round started, and I'll never forget that day if I live to be five hundred years old. It was the longest day I have ever known. Try as I would, concentrate as I would, I simply couldn't make that mashie work. I was out the first nine in forty-four—several strokes above what I should have taken. I managed to steady down on the homeward journey, and by sinking some long putts got a thirty-five, giving me seventy-nine for the round. This wasn't so bad, but in the afternoon I got steadily worse with this club, and finally, when I came to the last hole, a short pitch with the mashie, I took a seven and was thrown into a twelve-man tie for last place. If I had missed one of those long putts I got down, I would have failed to qualify and would have been out of the tournament then and there. It was the closest call I ever expected to have. I managed to slip through the next morning, and won my first match. But I was still way off, and the next day I had my hardest battle on: a thirty-six-hole match with Francis Ouimet, who had been playing brilliantly.

FINDS THE CAUSE

So, late that afternoon, I called in the services of Bellwood, the Garden City professional. He watched me play a few shots and then called the turn. I thought I had been doing a number of things badly, but I was wrong in each guess. My fault lay in the fact that as I started my club back I bent my left wrist too far, breaking the swing. Almost at the top of the swing this left wrist, in place of remaining firm, would break in toward my body. It was a matter of only an inch in the swing, but it meant fifty yards in direction.

I went out and practised early next morning, partially corrected the fault, which had started to become a fixed habit, and managed to win.

Which reminds me that the best advice I can give when one gets suddenly off is to look up a competent professional and find the cause at once. If I hadn't started in correcting that mistake in the right way, by another ten days it would have been a fixed habit, and I would surely have been up against it for many months.

Don't let these bad habits grow on you. And don't take it for granted that you know enough to correct them unaided. I made this mistake in regard to my driving. At one time this was one of the strongest parts of my game. Then I became ambitious for even more distance and began overswinging, that is, bringing the club too far back and around. I added distance, but at the expense of direction; and before I suddenly realized where I stood, this overswinging had developed into a steady habit, and it **has** bothered me and affected my game ever since. As a result now my hands, drawn out of the plane of **the** swing, are forced up, and I am never sure just when I can master this fault. I simply waited **too** long **before** seeking some cure.

TWO UNUSUAL CASES

There are some features of returning to form which are logical, and others which are beyond any human reckoning.

At one time Walter J. Travis, who is one of the hardest students of golf that ever lived, got badly off his drive. He had drawn a spell, as I remember it, of topping the ball, and there seemed to be no remedy in sight. Travis tried out all the known systems, and when these failed, he took the case into his own hands. He began to experiment, and finally found that he got much better results by only partially addressing the ball; that is, in place of placing his club head directly back of the ball on the ground, the back swing was started from a less rigid position with the club head still in the air. This system is different from any other I have ever seen, but it gets the right results, as there are very few who are any straighter down the course than the famous veteran. The logic of this stroke seems to be, in his case, that the club head goes through in better shape, with less tendency to tighten up just before the impact.

Another remarkable case is that of James Braid, the great English professional.

Braid had been a fine golfer, but, although a big, powerful man, his main defect had been inability to get distance from the tee. This had cost him heavily, as it had put him at a big disadvantage when playing against long drivers. He had worked upon this fault and tried every known system to cure it, without success. And then, one morning, starting a round, to his great astonishment he found that he had overnight added twenty-five or thirty yards to his drive. It had simply come to him and he could find no reason or cause for the sudden change. Ever since he has been one of the longest drivers in the game, and to this day he doesn't know where this extra thirty yards down the course came from.

THREE MAIN FAULTS

There are three main causes for golfing faults that I have noted in my experience with the game.

The first is "looking up," or moving the head.

The second is swaying or shifting the body in advance of the arms, thereby spoiling the timing of the swing.

The third is loss of confidence in making a shot, especially upon the putting green.

The first of these is a combination of the physical and the mental. More bad shots are made from "looking up"—not looking at the ball—than any other one factor.

The explanation of this fault is an easy one: Mind controls muscle, and the mind, also, works much faster than the hands. At the top of the swing the mind has already finished its work in regard to hitting the ball, and has moved on ahead to the bunker to be carried or the green to be reached. And the mind, being in control of the situation and working faster than the hands, sends the head flying up in an effort to follow the flight of the ball even before it has been struck. The result is disaster. As the head comes up the club is jerked from the plane of its swing and the shot wrecked to a certainty.

SUGGESTING A REMEDY

"Yes, I know," says the average golfer, "that I ought to look at the ball. But how can I make myself look at it? I've made up my mind to look at the ball on shot after shot, only to find my head still jerked up in the same old way. What can I do to cure this fault?"

I know of but one answer, and that is the practice of concentration. Most golfers are willing enough to practise physically, but they never think of practising mentally. Practise controlling your mind just as you practise swinging a club; practise keeping your *mind* on the ball as well as your *eye;* practise forgetting that any space exists beyond the ball, and practise the *thought* that your work is done when you get the ball away from that one small spot.   How many golfers practise concentration?   Not one out of a hundred.   They expect it to develop naturally, and such a thing doesn't develop without aid any more than the swing would develop.

HARD WORK

I know how hard this practice is.   I have always thought that but for breaking this cardinal precept I might have had a very good chance to beat Hilton in 1911 at Apawamis—when the English champion carried away our chief amateur trophy.

In the morning round over the first eighteen holes I had been playing badly, and finished four down. Every one, including Hilton, considered the match all in and over.   But in the afternoon I started with a rush and won the first three holes, leaving myself only one down and well within reach.   At the next

THEN I BECAME AMBITIOUS FOR EVEN MORE

hole I had an easy two-foot putt to make to win my fourth straight hole and square the match.

I have always thought that if I had made that putt the odds would have been in my favour. Now in putting I make it a set rule to look at the ball until my club has struck the spot I am looking at. I have been able to do this by constant practice of concentration. But on this occasion I had a downhill putt and I was over anxious. And just before my club struck the ball I looked up, pushed the ball to the right of the cup, and missed the shot. This upset me for a moment, and I topped my drive at the next hole, losing it. The combination, coming suddenly, restored Hilton's confidence, which had been ebbing away, and he got going again, with the result that I was beaten three and two.

TWO OTHER FAULTS

"But suppose I am slicing, or hooking?" queries the duffer. "How am I to stop that? Just looking at the ball won't do it."

[43]

Well, looking at the ball will help. But the main fault here is bad timing, which results mostly from letting the body get away from control.

And in this connection I would like to add a tip—most golfers are too ambitious. They want to do all the work themselves, with their arms and body and feet and head, leaving nothing for the club. Now the club has its part in the game. It has its work to do just as well as the hands. So why not let it do its share of the labour?

Too many golfers bring into play entirely too many muscles. On short shots make the stroke as simple as possible, using only the hands and arms, keeping the body out of it. On longer shots let the arms and club do more work, and the body less.

In other words, practise playing the shot in easier, simpler fashion, without all that unnecessary lunge and twist. Let the arms pull the body through, in place of the body pushing the arms through—which latter is the worst thing in the world for timing.

These are faults that should be corrected by a

visit to a professional, for, as I remarked before, if left too long they develop into fixed habits. I know the case of one golfer who was a club champion and a state champion. He had been playing golf for over ten years, and had fallen into a steady, even game. He was especially dependable with the wood. And then, almost imperceptibly, he began to break his swing at the top. The fault gradually became worse, until he was pushing his hands a foot out of the right plane at the top of his swing, and he soon was unable to hit a ball off the tee.

This player then called in the club professional, but found by that time the habit had become fixed. The man worked for over a year, practising steadily, without helping his case. He seemed to be hypnotized. With no ball to hit at, his swing was perfect. But the moment the professional placed a ball on the tee, his hands would push the club up over his head and wreck the stroke. The professional finally gave him up in despair. The golfer at last corrected the fault by practising driving with first his left hand and then his right, and by then going back to a half swing, extending it gradually. But he had two years of nightmare before he got going again.

THE MATTER OF CONFIDENCE

Getting back on one's confidence is even more important than getting back on one's game. And in this phase of golf come the most interesting cases connected with the game. Confidence or lack of confidence, making or breaking a player, may come or go at a single shot.

In this connection the case of Walter J. Travis at Sandwich in 1904 is an interesting example.

Travis had gone over to compete in the British Amateur Championship, but across the water he wasn't given a look-in. No one thought he had a chance. He had been playing good golf, but about ten days before the tournament started he suddenly went wrong in his putting.

Having always been a good putter, and knowing

the value of putting in tournament play, this was a hard blow to the American's hope and dream. He worked for hours, tried out various stances and various grips and all the methods in sight, without effect. The day of the first competitive match in championship play drew on, and yet Travis was still floundering. He was unable to lay an approach putt close or to sink a short one. Something had happened to break that mystic link which joined confidence with his play. And then, on the day of the tournament, he threw aside his own putter in disgust and borrowed one from an American friend.

The first putt he tried for went down with a cluck. And from that point on Travis gave the greatest exhibition of putting any tournament has ever seen. He simply walked through the field of England's best, and he turned the trick by sinking the most wonderful putts that England had ever seen. A fifteen-footer was dead easy. He got most of the twenty-footers and, strange to say, about the only putts of any sort that he missed were the wee ones that he should have holed easily. Travis met Black-well in the final round and literally putted him to death. Blackwell would be five feet from the cup in three and Travis twenty feet in three. Travis would then sink his twenty-footer for a four, and the shock would upset the Englishman, who very often missed.

What had happened? Nothing except that Travis had suddenly recovered his confidence with a new putter.

ANOTHER COMMON FAULT

There is still another mistake which I have noted frequently while watching others play over various courses. And this fault is especially common among the so-called duffers.

You see them playing up and down the course, missing their iron shots, topping most of them, and wondering what on earth has happened. It's quite easy to detect the cause. When they want to get the ball up in the air, in place of letting the club, which is built for that purpose, do the work, they attempt to get the ball up by jerking their hands up

[48]

as if they were doing the lifting. The iron face of a mashie, mashie-niblick, jigger, and mid-iron is constructed for the purpose of getting the ball in the air.

If the club head comes through properly, the ball will rise in the proper way. But a big section of the golfing clan doesn't seem to appreciate this. They feel that they must snap their wrists up as the club head meets the ball, to get the ball up. This is almost sure to result in a topped shot—certainly in a bad one. So, when you have a spell of topping with your irons, recall this, and begin to let the club head do the lifting. Let the club head go on through, and by no means make any attempt to jerk the ball up from its lie. This is a notorious fault and one that will bear watching, for it spoils many a shot in the course of a season, almost as many as looking up or shifting the body into poor timing.

A USEFUL HINT

One of the main things for a golfer to remember in

starting to get back on his game is that golf, above all other things in the world, is a game of infinite patience.

Those who expect too much, who are looking for quick returns, worry too much, get peevish, and finally careless. In place of working more easily than usual and with more thought, they hit harder and harder, and let their tempers wreck their judgment. The only chance a golfer has to correct a fault is to secure the proper instruction, and then work at his comeback with patience and with deliberate thought. It is impossible to say how many golfers have been ruined by expecting too much in too short a time, and then letting discouragement set in.

I was playing in a two-ball match one day with a veteran golfer. We passed another golfer on the course who had been playing less than a year. We were right at him when he stepped up to a pitch shot over the bunker and then foozled, with the result that he carried nicely into trouble.

The aftermath was an explosion. He threw his club after the ball, and began to get profane in about five languages at the same time.

When he had finished his long list of expletives my friend, the veteran player, simply said, "What's the kick? You didn't expect to make a good shot, did you?"

And the profanity started all over again. But that was the trouble. The duffer saw no reason why he shouldn't make that shot like an Evans. And when he failed, instead of realizing that it was only natural that a beginner should miss a hard pitch shot of that type, he immediately flew into a frenzy, and probably got worse and worse. Suppose, in place of losing control of his temper there, that he had taken things as a matter of course, and put the same amount of energy into studying just what he had done wrong, and in thinking of some way to correct the fault. He would not only have found greater pleasure in the game, but he would have begun to improve beyond the average.

I cite this case because it is illustrative of a big body of golfers—an amazing percentage. Here we have a game that requires more calmness, judgment, stolidity, and control than any other game ever known—for the player here is at all times playing against himself—his own weakness. And yet we have thousands of players trying to learn it with frazzled nerves, with their tempers unleashed, with their judgment wrecked, simply because they haven't been able to control themselves, and all the while they are wondering why it is they don't improve and why it is they can't possibly "get back on their game." How can a man get back to a given point when he starts in exactly the opposite direction from that point? He might possibly do so by travelling around the world, but in no other way.

Any man with an average athletic tendency can get back on his game in golf if he will only follow a few set rules and regulations:

If he will first seek competent instruction.

If he will then practise concentration, and practise thoroughly the art of thinking how the stroke should be played.

If he will practise control of his temper and his judgment and will keep a clear head, working with patience and calmness.

I know this is easier to write than it is to do. But if a golfer finds it beyond his mental powers to follow this route he is in for a hard time of it, unless he is an exceptional genius, and he is quite sure to find that he will spend the greater part of his time "all off his game, simply unable to get going again." Life for him then will be just one alibi after another. He had better quit the sport entirely, and save his own nerves and the nerves of his friends.

SONG OF THE NINETEENTH HOLE

A blear-eyed golfer landed home at 3 o'clock one morn,

About six down, or maybe more, to old J. Barleycorn;

And when he looked around and saw between him and
his bed

His spouse had laid a stymie with a rolling pin, he said—

"I'm sorry, dear, that I'm so late—I know that I'm
to blame—

But I have been out playing bonny Scotland's grand
old game";

Whereat she seized the rolling pin with still a firmer clutch,

And showed him by this chorus that the Duffer was in
Dutch—

Chorus:

"I know about your golf, old boy, where twenty drinks
are par;

How all your short approaches leave you close against
the bar;

You move along from cup to cup until you're orey-eyed;

The only Scotch game you can play has soda on the side."

In vain the wretched golfer took an oath upon his death;

In vain—because he could not put a back spin on his breath;

In vain he foozled each excuse and topped each alibi,

Until at last he played himself into a wretched lie;

He said that he'd been "pressing" and he spoke of "perfect form,"

To find that he was standing in the pathway of a storm;

The lady took a Vardon grip upon that rolling pin,

And as she took a Ouimet swing she said above the din—

Chorus:

"I know about your golf, old boy, where twenty drinks are par"— etc.

III

WONDER SHOTS THAT WON GOLF CHAMPIONSHIPS

I HAVE watched a ball game and at some critical point I have seen a home batsman lash out a two-base hit just beyond some infielder's reach, scoring the winning run. And I have thought that I was thrilled to the limit.

I have watched football games, and at some close stage have seen a fast halfback suddenly swing loose, dash past all opposition except one lone man playing well back, and as this lone tackler dived for his man I was still sure that I was thrilled to the limit of things.

But at Brookline, Massachusetts, where America's Open Golf Championship was under way, I found that I had never been thrilled before—that I had just discovered what the word thrill really means.

[56]

We were standing around the eighteenth green that Friday afternoon, knowing that Vardon and Ray, the great English players, had tied for first place, when word came in that young Francis Ouimet, the fine young Massachusetts amateur, was still in the fight and with a bare outside chance to tie the two English stars.

The story of that remarkable finish, where Ouimet accomplished the miraculous, has already become old in the telling, but there are two shots concerning which I do not believe that "the half has ever been told." To my mind these two putts outlined the most wonderful golfing psychology that the game has ever known in all its history. And before I take these two shots up I should like somewhat further to illustrate the psychological possibilities of the occasion from a section of my own golfing experience.

No one who hasn't been through it can ever appreciate the strain that comes in the winning of a first championship. It is almost unbearable, and has broken many golfers who might have added the title to their achievements.

MY FIRST CHAMPIONSHIP

My first championship came over the Euclid course at Cleveland, Ohio, in 1907. In the final round of that affair, playing against Archie Graham, I had come to the thirteenth hole in the afternoon with the lead of five up and but six to play. I had to win but one more hole of the remaining six to be champion. I had to halve but two holes to be champion. Yet when I came to my last putt on the thirteenth green I almost cracked. I had only a four-foot putt to make in order to win, and even if I missed it I would be dormie five. I felt that day that I couldn't make that putt if I had to be shot. I told Graham so. "Oh, drop it in," he remarked, "and end the agony. You couldn't miss it with your eyes shut."

I got the putt, but I was surprised when it dropped in. Now I am not supposed to be afflicted with any great amount of nervousness, but here was a putt that was not at all vital or important, but which came near upsetting me because I realized that a championship was so close. I am using this case to illustrate the remarkable psychology involved in those two putts by Ouimet last fall.

TWO WORLD BEATERS

When Ouimet had finished the sixteenth hole he still had a three and a four left for a tie with the two Britons. And a three on the eighteenth hole was next to impossible except by a fluke, so he had to get a three on the seventeenth. Now the seventeenth green at Brookline is a most treacherous affair, or was that day, with a decided slope and as fast as a streak. Probably the strongest part of my game is putting, and that green had got well upon my nerves and had me guessing.

On his second shot that day Ouimet planted his ball on the green about twenty feet from the cup and above the hole. It was almost impossible to get close to the cup on your second shot here, as the hole was close to a bunker that would have meant disaster in case of any deviation from an almost perfect line. So Ouimet had to play above and to the right of the hole, leaving the hardest of all putting combinations: a downhill, sidehill putt. It was about as difficult a putt as a man was ever called upon to make. Under the circumstances it was almost beyond hope. There was hardly a chance for him to lay dead. If he missed the cup over the fast, tricky green, he was almost sure to go five or six feet below and have another hard putt for a four. And even a four there would have been useless.

Ouimet knew this, and he must have figured just what it meant. But even though I knew he had a wonderful temperament for golf, I was surprised to note the sure, easy, and confident way he went to that putt. I recalled my own experience of six years before. Yet here was a kid of twenty—without a flutter. He went for the cup as if he had been trying a practice putt. Over the wet, slippery green rolled to a fast smoothness the ball started on a perfect line, curved in at exactly the right spot, and struck the back of the cup with as welcome a cluck-cluck as I have ever heard.

But that wasn't all. He had gotten his three on a par four hole—the hole that next day cost Vardon any chance for the championship, as the Englishman took a five there—but there was still another hole to play and a hard one, calling for fine golf to register the needed four. Ouimet had a good drive and played a fine second shot over a road guarding the green to the edge of the bank, where the ball struck in the rain-soaked turf and stopped dead. There was a dip in the green between his ball and the cup with the hole up the slope. On this shot I would have used a putter to follow the roll of the ground and get up fairly close. But Ouimet elected to use a mashie, and when he pitched, the ball landed six or seven feet short—not an exceptionally long distance away, but the most trying distance imaginable when one needs that putt badly. He had already wriggled out of one close call and was up against another—one shot left to tie Britain's two golfing kings and keep his country on the golfing map. It was that one shot, or America passed, to let England fight out America's championship on American soil.

The nervous strain here must have been even greater than it was upon the previous hole. There he was, with three thousand of his countrymen looking on and praying for his success. I have never seen an occasion so charged with excitement. The air was rife with it, and you could feel suppressed emotion darting about like currents of electricity. Again I recalled my experience of six years before and the nervous flutter I felt where everything was in my favour, and I wondered if a human lived who could hold his poise in Ouimet's place. With me, it wasn't so much the fact that he made the putt as it was the way he went about it. There was no sign of any sort of nervousness. He walked up to his ball with an easy, steady stride, barely took a look at the hole, wasted no time in getting set, and with three thousand of his followers almost breaking apart under the strain, he putted boldly for the center with a clean, free tap that could have come only from muscles under perfect mental control.

And when that putt dropped, I realized then that I had never felt a regular thrill before—that the others were all counterfeits.

A RECORD PUTT

From the viewpoint of psychology these two putts of Ouimet's were the most wonderful I ever saw. But from the physical side of things I once saw Walter J. Travis, the veteran, sink the most wonderful putt it has ever been my lot to witness.

The occasion was a Metropolitan Championship at Garden City with Travis and Wilder of Boston in a hard match. Travis was four down and four to play, hanging on by a thin thread of hope. But Travis settled down and won the fifteenth and sixteenth holes, leaving himself only two down with two holes left. He had to win both, of course, to even get a half. But his rally seemed to be fading out at the seventeenth hole, and those who had wagered four to one against Wilder—one man I know had bet two hundred dollars to fifty on Travis—were looking on with sick expressions. For all Wilder needed was a half here to win the match. And after playing three shots he was only four feet from the cup. And Travis on his third shot was barely on the green, thirty feet away.

The battle seemed to be over beyond any hope, for Travis was not only thirty feet away, but he had one of the trickiest and hardest greens on the course to putt over. And even if he made the putt the odds were that Wilder would also make his from that distance. Travis had no chance to try for a straight putt. There were two decided breaks in the slope of the green, one to the left and one to the right. And between these two mounded slopes there was a narrow gap between knolls. It was impossible to follow the line of this gap because the cup was set back of a knoll to the left, blocking entrance in that direction.

He had only one way to go, and that was to take

the mounded slope to the right. The Old Man walked up to the cup and studied the line carefully from that angle. Then he walked slowly back, studying the lay of the ground along the line he must take. He had to figure all this tricky slope to the inch, and to the inch for thirty feet. For any slight break off the right line would probably put him three or four feet away at the finish.

After a careful survey he walked back to his putt and with a free tap sent the ball spinning along. It took the slope to the right, wound its way along this raised mound and, winding, turning, twisting up-slope and down-slope, it broke in at exactly the right spot, about twenty-eight feet away, and it then plumped squarely into the center of the cup, taking its last run from a decided downhill spin where the green sloped off abruptly toward the hole. I've never seen another like it.

The effect was so startling that Wilder, being human, promptly missed his four-footer and then lost the next hole, leaving the match all square. He rallied after this and fought an even fight at the thirty-seventh, thirty-eighth, and thirty-ninth holes, but at the fortieth Travis sank another hard putt for one under par and won the match.

TAYLOR'S ESCAPE

These long putts are sometimes necessary to save one's fate. In fact, the occasion develops rather frequently in championship play.

At Hoylake, in the British Open, J. H. Taylor, the crack English pro., found himself up against a similar proposition. Now Vardon had won the British Open on five occasions and Braid had won it on five occasions. Taylor had won only four times, and he was, of course, highly keyed up with the idea and with the hope that he might tie his famous opponents. This tournament was played in a hard rain coupled with a driving wind—the severest test known. And before the seventy-two-hole medal round started, the field was so large that it was necessary to have a qualifying round where only a certain proportion, those among the best twenty in each group, could qualify.

In this qualifying round Taylor had failed to strike his gait. He had been a trifle off. So much so, in fact, that it looked for one shaky moment as if he wouldn't qualify. Taylor had come to the last green and the finish with but one shot left to get in and get a chance to continue. If he missed this putt he was out of it for good, out among the discards. He was twenty feet away from the cup when he started his putt. The ball trickled on, came to rest at the edge, hung there for an interminable length of time and finally wobbled over in for the needed four. And after that narrow squeak, where the odds were five to one against him, Taylor went out and won the British Open Championship for the fifth time, tying the records set up by Harry Vardon and James Braid.

TREED?—NOT QUITE

I believe two of the best shots I ever made were both pulled off under similar conditions. The first one was at Baltusrol, the second at Englewood, and both were in Metropolitan Championships. In each case, with hard matches on, against Seeley first and Byers later on, my ball had come to rest just in front of a tree with the hole on beyond. There was no chance to shoot straight for the cup, as I was unable to get my club back without striking the tree. To play safe was useless, for I had to reach the green even to get a half. So on each occasion I took a desperate chance, standing with my back almost to the hole. To play the shot from this stance I had to play almost at right angles to the green, allowing for a terrific pull. On each occasion I swept my club around, put my wrists sharply into the shot, and in some way managed to engineer sufficient hook to save the hole.

There were two other shots that saved me in one of my toughest matches. They came at Garden City against Ouimet in the Amateur Championship. He had been playing at top speed, and I knew that I had a battle under way early. At the finish of the morning round I was one up. But Ouimet started off briskly in the afternoon, caught me soon, and after leaving the seventh hole was one up. Playing the eighth hole we were about alike on our drives, and he followed with a fine long pitch to the green, only eight feet from the cup. I saw then that the situation was becoming serious. If he won this hole he would be two up with only ten holes left, and at the clip he was travelling this would leave me in a dangerous fix. I knew, after he had made this last shot, that he figured the hole won— that he was practically two up. I saw also that I had a chance here to jar some of his confidence loose by turning the tables. So I put all the psychology and wrist play I had into my shot, landing only three feet from the pin. He then missed, I holed out for a three, and was all square in place of being two down. I won the ninth hole and we halved the tenth, leaving me one up. He made another bid at the eleventh, where his second shot was only twelve feet from the cup. This time I took another chance of driving a blow home, and from one hundred and forty yards away planted the ball within two feet of the pin. But the shot that turned the tide, as Ouimet admitted later on, came at the eighth hole.

THE HEAVY STRAIN

It is remarkable in golf how often one shot will win or lose a match. Most people fail to appreciate the abnormal strain, both physical and mental, under which the player must fight his way through the field. I once knew a star football player, a guard weighing over two hundred pounds, who had never taken out time in his football career. He was a glutton for hard work, and was always able to finish even a big battle in fine condition. After finishing college he began to pay more attention to golf, which he had played at intervals only before. In one of the big championships toward the finish of the tournament he almost collapsed under the strain, playing so badly that he was beaten easily. He told me afterward that he had never believed it possible that a game like golf would send him to the mat where he had been able to survive football without a flutter.

The difference is this: in football the player suffers only from physical weariness; but in golf the mental strain is so great that unless a man has absolute control of his nerves, they become raw and leave him a nervous wreck for the time being. Two days after a football or baseball season is over the players are generally feeling fit. But last fall it was several weeks before Ouimet recovered from his Brookline experience, and at the end of the season J. J. McDermott, one of the greatest professionals in the country, broke down and had to take over a month's rest.

If a man hasn't almost complete control over his nervous system he will never win a championship. Vardon, Braid, and Taylor, the great British golfers, who have each won the British Open five times, are all masters of their temperament. They have learned to take the game as it comes—to accept their fate without a complaint. If they miss a shot, you will never see any one of them bat an eyelash. They know what it means to keep an unruffled temper and to be possessed of some reserve force to fall back upon at the time when needed.

FREAKS OF NERVOUS FORCE

This nervous force works in queer and mysterious systems. There are some people who are highly nervous in medal rounds, but who become steady when they swing into match play. I never do nearly as well in a medal round as I do in a match round. On the other hand, the system works exactly the opposite with Charles Evans, Jr., Chicago's young star. Evans can literally eat a medal round alive, taking it without a quiver. But in match play he is generally below form. In 1912, at Wheaton, Harold Hilton had led the field in the medal round with a seventy-five. Evans was the only one left to tie the English champion. He had a four left to tie at the final hole. This hole is over four hundred yards long, and Evans, after a bad tee shot, had to play his second far wide of the green to get out at all. This left him a high, difficult pitch over some trees to reach the green in three and have a chance for his four. He executed the pitch perfectly, with wonderful nerve and judgment, and landed on the green twenty feet away. Then, although not a steady putter, he walked up and sank his putt for a four.

He had mastered the nerves of medal round. But at match play, when we met in the thirty-sixth-hole final, he was not the same. Evans has won five out of his last seven starts at medal play in the Amateur Championship, but has yet to win the match-play championship. And while I have won the championship on four occasions, I have never even figured in a medal round. Which shows how apart the two systems are and what different types of golf are required to meet the two occasions.

When this lack of confidence arrives, the golfer is in a bad way. At Garden City last fall, Evans was playing against E. M. Byers, of Pittsburgh. For the greater part of that first round Evans had mastered his weakness on the green, had recovered confidence, and was going along as only Evans can when he swings into his best stride. At the seventeenth hole he was six up on Byers, with the match well in hand. Playing the eighteenth the Chicago golfer pitched to within ten feet of the cup. Byers was twenty-five feet away. On his approach putt Byers ran six feet over and missed coming back, netting a four. Evans had two putts to win and three to halve. He hit the cup for a two, but caromed four feet away, and finally took three putts from that distance, losing the hole with a five.

This sudden recurrence of bad putting got upon his nerves again with the result that, while still five up, Evans lost this margin within the next nine or ten holes, and finally had a thirty-eight-hole battle ahead before he could win. That one hole had cost him all this extra nervous strain, and he was still unsettled from his strenuous experience next day when he met J. G. Anderson, and was beaten in the semi-final round. If he had been able to have made that one short putt he would have finished his morning round seven up, and more than likely would have won with ease in the afternoon, thereby being able to reserve his nervous force for a better showing next day.

THE EFFECT OF ONE SHOT

The effect of one good shot or one bad shot is often startling. In the Metropolitan Open Championship, held at Englewood in 1911, Gilbert Nicholls was playing his last nine holes. He got a four on the tenth, playing at only a steady clip up through here. The eleventh hole there is four hundred yards along. Nicholls put away a good drive, and on his second shot used a mid-iron. The ball started on a line for the cup, and a second later a shout came from those around the green. He had holed in two from one hundred and sixty yards away! From that point no golfer that ever lived could have touched him. He finished the nine in thirty, breaking all previous records by two strokes and winning the championship in a walk. After that one two he picked up two other holes in two, playing with such confidence and daring that it seemed as if he couldn't miss from any distance.

One year at Brookline, in the American Open, I followed one of the leading professionals competing there. He had been moving along steadily until he finally came to one of the most treacherous greens. The hole was a long one, over four hundred yards. His drive was a beauty. He played a wonderful second shot on the green about four feet above the cup. He had this putt for a three. If he could make this hard hole in three, he would probably be off on an inspiration dash, a hard man to head off. The green was as fast as lightning and the putt was downhill. He putted, missed, and the ball, like a man grasping for a hold as he rolls down an embankment, twisted and rolled on by the cup and travelled twenty feet before it stopped. He took three putts to get back in the cup. In place of getting á three he got a six, and from that point on faded out of the championship fight. That one shot had destroyed all his confidence, had given him a deadly fear of the greens, and he was through.

THE UPSET

Some years ago I found out what a shock arrives when the other fellow does the unexpected. I was playing one of my first big matches with Walter J. Travis at Garden City. He was a veteran then and I a kid. We finished the first thirty-six holes all square. We halved the thirty-seventh, and at the thirty-eighth I pitched on the green within ten feet of the cup, while Travis overplayed into the bunker beyond. I considered the match over then and there. It had been a grinding one all the way, and I could already taste the sweets of victory. Then I got my first shock: Travis played from the bunker within a foot of the hole, dead for a three. I was more than shocked. I tried for my two, missed, and overran, and then missed my three, losing hole and match.

That taught me a lesson—not to consider any hole won or lost until the ball was in the cup. I've never forgotten it.

Possibly the hardest upset that ever developed came at Apawamis in 1911, when Harold Hilton of England and Fred Herreshoff of Garden City fought out the championship round. They were all even at the end of thirty-six holes. The thirty-seventh hole, which naturally is also number one, is located upon a high green, bordered at the right by a towering rock, almost a cliff. Both drives were down the middle, but Herreshoff had the best shot, within easy pitching of the green. Hilton, therefore, had to play first. His shot, badly sliced, travelled off to the right, and the match looked to be over, with America on top. For it seemed as if nothing could keep that ball from bounding off from the cliff into an almost unplayable spot. Herreshoff, after the grinding journey, must have thought the same, and so must have felt that at last his work was done. But by some strange freak the ball struck a projection from the side of the rock and caromed off upon the green for a sure four in place of an almost sure six. The upset to Herreshoff was quite natural and his approach was bad, costing him the hole and championship.

One of the most fatal single shots that I have ever seen was played by Heinrich Schmidt at Garden City in the last Amateur Championship. Schmidt had done wonderful work in the English Amateur and was well touted for this tournament. His first round was badly played, the eighteen holes costing him eighty-six. He steadied down in his second journey, however, and came through with seventy-nine. This left him tied for first place with twelve of us who had also required one hundred and sixty-five for the thirty-six-hole test. Then we all started in to play the next extra hole, where twelve of the thirteen were to qualify, with only one to be dropped out. The main object here, of course, was to play safe. Schmidt had one of the best drives of the lot, and before it came his time to play a second shot he had seen two others go into the deep bunker or trap guarding the green.

All he had to do here was to be sure of getting well over, even if he overran the green. But in place of this he used a niblick, tried for a most difficult pitch, and fell short in the worst sort of trouble, putting him out of the tournament. As he was coming back upon his game at a lively clip he might have had a good chance, but faulty judgment left him at the post.

Golf is full of single chances of this nature, where one shot may win or lose and where calm judgment and control of nerves are necessary to achieve the right result. There is no actual physical contest of man against man, but there is a heart-tearing contest of nerve against nerve all the way, and the one who comes through safely must hold himself perfectly in hand. For it is hard enough to keep the pace at a normal clip at a crucial spot, much less rise to the occasion with a phenomenal shot that decides the day's issue.

But one of these phenomenal or unexpected shots always works with double force. It not only gives the one who makes it greater hope and confidence, but it comes as a hard shock to the other man who had considered the hole won.

A 269-YARD CARRY

There is still another class of golf shots, not so interesting, as they lack the mental side, but wonderful from the physical power required. An example is the shot Ed Ray played at the sixteenth hole at Shawnee. This hole is about two hundred and sixty-eight yards from the tee. It is guarded by a deep brook, and beyond the brook a decided uphill slope. Before Ray came up, Vardon, McDermott, and Alec Smith, all long hitters, took drivers and, after clean wallops, struck the side of the bank and fell short. The shot had to be nearly all carry, as the ground was soft from recent rains and the uphill slope prevented much run. When Ray stepped up, he took a look at the hole and then stepped back, called his caddie, and replaced his driver, taking out a cleek. The crowd around gasped—and then laughed. But Ray knew what he was about. Weighing two hundred and twenty pounds, with broad, sloping shoulders that denote great physical power, he ranks among the longest drivers in the world. With a tremendous swipe he hurled the head of that cleek into the ball, and when it landed on a full carry the white pill was within ten feet of the cup. He had carried brook, slope, and everything else in the way with a cleek, where other long players had failed with a club that is supposed to get twenty yards more distance.

But, after all, it is the shot played with the brain and heart rather than with the arm and shoulder that counts most.

THE DUFFER'S REQUIEM
(*With Apologies to R. L. S.*)

Under the wide and starry sky
Dig the grave and let me lie;
Gladly I've lived and gladly die
Away from the world of strife;
These be the lines you grave for me:
"Here he lies where he wants to be;
Lies at rest by the nineteenth tee,
Where he lied all through his life."

THE RIME OF THE ANCIENT GOLFER
'Conceding Two Strokes to Colonel Coleridge)

It was an ancient Golfer,
    And he stoppeth one of three;
" By thy baffing spoon, thou crazy loon,
    Now wherefore stoppest me?"

He held me with his glittering eye,
I had to get that alibi.

" I drove them straight from every tee—
    I soaked them on the crest;
I played my mashie like a Braid
    Or Vardon at his best.

" But eke when I had reached the green
    I was a pie-eyed mutt;
I would have had a 68
    If I could only putt.

[84]

"I putted slow—I putted fast—

I made them roll and hop;

I putted standing up and crouched,

But still they would not drop.

"About—about in reel and rout

My score went on the blink;

Aye, putters, putters everywhere,

But not a putt would sink.

"I hit the cup eleven times

And rimmed it seven more;

I bit my arm, I shrieked aloud,

I wept and then I swore;

I should have had a 68,

But got a 94."

I left that crazy loon and ran

As any one would do,

And hustled off to tell a guy

About the putts I blew,

How I deserved a 66

But got a 92.

IV

THE SECRET OF STEADY GOLF

GOLF is overrun with mysteries and queer shifts because it carries more of the psychological than any other game. But of them all, here is probably the main puzzle that has been put up to me in queries by any number of people:

"Why is it that I can go out upon a certain day feeling perfectly fit in every way and play a most wretched game, while on other days, feeling out of sorts and in no condition to play well, my scores are unexpectedly low?"

These peculiar conditions have probably confronted every man that ever followed the ancient Scottish game, for they form a part of the eternal question put forward by so many golfers all over the world: "Why is it that I can play so well upon some days—and so badly upon others? What is there in this game of golf that keeps the player so uncertain of his showing, regardless of his mental and physical feelings for the day?''

AIDS AND SUGGESTIONS

There is no set answer, of course, to the "Secret of Steady Golf" that might always fit in; but I believe there are certain aids and suggestions which will help wonderfully if properly followed out.

In the first place, there are two features of golf which must be considered, above the mere ability of a player to play a certain shot. There are any number who can stand upon a tee in practice, and make shot after shot like a Vardon, Ray, or Taylor. But once out in the wear and tear of active competition they are all over the course without a shot left. These two main features, mentioned before, are Nerve and Control of Nerve—quite separate and distinct, but entirely too often confused.

It not only takes Nerve to win at golf, but in

addition the complete control of nerves. There are men who have raw courage enough to charge a lion's den, but who haven't control of nerves enough to make a three-foot putt in a tight match. Nerves must be used as something more than the plural of Nerve, as used in the sporting sense. The two are not the same.

CONTROL OF NERVES

"But how," asks the duffer, "can I get this control of nerves?"

How do you learn to play a mashie or to putt? For the most part by practice. And that is how one must learn control of nerves—by practising this matter of control just as one practises swinging a club. The golfer must learn how to get a grip upon himself, and he can learn this by practising the development of that rarest of all aids to good golf—concentration.

There is one thing that has helped me more in match play than any other factor, and that is *to play each shot by itself—to forget what has gone before and*

LIFTING THE BALL WITH THE BODY AND ARMS—
NOT LETTING THE CLUB DO THE LIFTING

think only of the shot immediately before you. This faculty didn't come naturally or easily. It came only through hard practice in concentration, practice that came harder than learning how to use a mashie or a putter, for it wasn't as real and as much before me.

AN EXAMPLE

Here's an example of what I mean: One summer at Baltusrol I was playing Oswald Kirkby in the final round of the Jersey State Championship.

In the afternoon we had come to the thirteenth hole, neck and neck, after the hardest sort of a match. This hole is about 220 yards long, the drive being over a deep ditch about 160 yards from the tee. Kirkby played and got a beautiful shot to the edge of the green. I topped my shot, and when I found the ball, discovered it just halfway down the embankment. The hole looked to be all over, for I was in an almost unplayable position, as it was raining and I could get no stance.

If I had fretted over missing my tee shot or bothered about the lie of the ball I wouldn't have had a chance. But I had only one thought in mind, and that was the next shot ahead—the shot left to get that ball somewhere and someway out of the ditch. I took a niblick, swung down hard, and then had to jump to keep from slipping as I made the shot. I almost had to hit the ball while I was still in mid-air, jumping over the ditch. I got it out, regardless of distance, and then found I had played far over the green into a high and heavy patch of grass beyond. The only thought I had then was still the next shot, how to get out of that young wheatfield back on the green in three. It was not up to me to pay any attention to the fact that my opponent was on the edge in one. It was only up to me to get as close to the hole as I could in three, since I already had played two strokes. I finally got on twelve feet below the cup in three and ran down my four. It was a hard green to putt on and conditions were bad, so when Kirkby finally needed a four I had drawn a half.

Now if I had wasted any time in bothering or

worrying about the trouble I had got in, I wouldn't have had a chance. But the part that helped me was the old practice of concentration, of concentrating exclusively on the shot ahead and not the mistake behind. This concentration isn't coming to you with a whistle. It is only coming by hard work, by mental application, by drilling yourself. But when it does come it will be of invaluable aid.

LOOK TO THE GAME—NOT THE ALIBI

Here's another point—make a practice of taking each lie as you find it, without blaming your bad luck. I watched Harry Vardon carefully, and I noticed that his expression never changed, whether his ball was lying badly or well set up. You must make up your mind that all bad lies are a part of golf, an expected part, and that they are coming to you in every round. Bad luck, like good luck, is a part of the game, and there will be enough good luck to offset the bad if you will only stop and look back at the end of the round.

[91]

Look at the game itself, the game as it comes, not to the alibi, or excuse for making a **bad** shot.

THE CASE OF JIMMY ALLEN

The first year that Vardon won the British Open the British Amateur was held at Muirfield, Scotland. One of the amateur entries was a youngster known as Jimmy Allen. He lived a good many miles from the course, and being poor he had to walk over every morning to play. He was so poor, in fact, that he didn't have money enough to buy nails for his shoes to prevent him from slipping. He had only a few old clubs in his bag, but among them he had neither a driver nor a putter. Before the championship started, he borrowed an old driver from the club professional and decided to do his putting with his cleek.

Now here was a golfer who had every alibi in the world to offer. He had to walk a good many miles to reach the course, play in shoes without a hobble, drive with a borrowed driver, and putt on fast greens with a cleek.

[92]

But he wasn't thinking of an alibi, or an excuse, or worrying about his luck. His entire mind was concentrated on winning that championship and playing the best golf he knew how to play. And at the end of the week he was amateur golf champion of Great Britain.

He had fine ability, of course. But it was ability working under a handicap that would have stopped most others from even considering the thought of entering the tournament. He not only entered, but he took his slippery shoes, borrowed driver, and transformed cleek as a part of the game, and won.

GOLF TEMPERAMENTS

This all, of course, gets back to golf temperaments. Concentration is far easier for some golfers than it is for others. The two finest golf temperaments in America I have ever known belong to Walter J. Travis and young Francis Ouimet.

It isn't given to every golfer to have the Ouimet temperament—a gift in his case, because he is too young to have developed it so thoroughly—the temperament to know that you have to play the last four holes one under par to tie two masters—and to do it with about as much strain as one would require to eat a scrambled egg.

I have heard it said that Ouimet in that match was dazed, and so was numb to the strain. On the other hand, he wasn't any more upset or worried than if he had been off by himself playing a few practice shots. It isn't for every man to have or to develop the Travis or the Ouimet temperament, but he can at least greatly improve his own by mental application, by schooling his mind or brain just as he schools his hands and arms and feet. And he must keep at it until it is fixed through force of habit, just as the stance and the grip are fixed. Thinking about it once in a while won't do any good. He must keep at it until control is fairly well established, and if he does he will be surprised to find how much steadier his game is growing, and how much strain is lifted from him through a round.

THE SECRET OF STEADY GOLF

OUIMET'S SYSTEM

Ouimet has cultivated the system of entering each hard match with the idea uppermost that he will take the game as it comes. "I believe," he says, "that it is bad policy to start a hard match too optimistic— too confident in your success. For then, if the tide turns against you, if you meet unexpected opposition, you are much more likely to start worrying. Lack of confidence is of course fatal. The thing to do is not to think about the result any more than possible, but to play each shot as it comes.

"In my match against Vardon and Ray for the American Open I felt I had a faint chance to win, until about the fifth or sixth hole, when a bad shot gave me my first of expectancy. At this hole I hooked a shot out of bounds. This misplay cost only **one** stroke. If the shot had remained in bounds it would have been in an almost unplayable strip of woods, and would have certainly cost me heavily. As it was I got a half, and for the first time felt that

I was on my way; but I still stuck to my own game rather than theirs."

REPRESSED ENERGY

Golf is an entirely different game from baseball, football, or tennis. These are all contests of constant action, where nervous energy can help drive the player forward and keep him at top speed. But golf is a game of repressed energy. And that in the main is the answer to the question as to why a player, feeling unfit, often does unexpectedly well, and on the next day, primed for a fine round, does very poorly.

On the first occasion his energy is dormant. His nerves, tired down, are at rest. There are no jumping, ambitious nerves to repress. He doesn't look up as badly, for he doesn't care enough where the shot goes. The result is relaxation and an easy, natural attitude, for, not caring or feeling in the mood to care, the player isn't working under any strain.

But if he goes out expecting to play well, feeling fit for it, the odds are that his nerves are very much alive and will soon get the best of the battle, causing him to look up from the ball frequently through over-eagerness to follow the result of the shot.

A player takes one stance and one grip for each club as he starts his round, and he must practise the knack of taking, as far as possible, one mental attitude—the attitude of ease and control, of concentration upon the work ahead.

BUSINESS MAN

To the man in business, one engrossed with other matters, this concentration or steadiness can rarely be developed beyond a certain limit. For golf is a jealous mistress. You may notice how certain stars come forward, go into business, and then disappear from the winning ranks. This isn't only because they haven't quite as much time to play and practise, but also because the constant attention and thought they were once devoting to golf has been divided, and they find it difficult to keep on concentrating in a hard, close match.

This may not affect his long game, but it is sure to count in the short game, and especially in putting. A business man, worried and bothered over business details, may think that he can go out on the course and entirely forget his troubles. But the subconscious effect is still there, and his game is sure to show it. He may forget on the surface, but the forgetting won't go very deep, and his score will soon begin to mount.

Professionals give their entire time to golf, and, therefore, for the most part, rule the field. It isn't so much because they can play certain strokes any better, but because they have developed a greater steadiness, with little else to divert their attention from the game on or off the course. But what the business man can do is to improve conditions by practising shifting his concentration from business to golf, often a hard thing to do. For two seasons I was engaged in work not especially attractive to me, more or less nagging, and while I played a good bit of golf, I dropped completely out of the championship hunt. I was unable to concentrate as I had formerly done, and this helped put me out of it early.

A HINT FROM VARDON

The average golfer in England is far steadier than the average golfer in America, because over there the average golfer is willing to practise harder, while over here most of the golfers have no patience for anything except to play around the course in friendly rivalry with some opponent.

Every golfer that ever played has at times felt the curse of unsteadiness in his game, the absence of touch or of something that was vital to the right stroke. But the world's record for unsteadiness probably goes to a certain California golfer. There was a team match scheduled between two clubs, each club picking its five best men. When the match started it was discovered that only four men had reported for one of the teams. The captain of the team that had a missing man saw, standing by, a club member with a handicap somewhere around 16 or 18 strokes.

His average game was about 98. As a rule he could be counted upon to go out in 50 and come back in 48. That day, to his own amazement and to the confusion of his opponent, he was out in 34—eleven strokes better than he had ever played the course before for the first nine holes. This was an upset, but no worse than the upset that followed, for, after being out in 34, he was back in 63. He got his 97, but as no 97 was ever gotten before.

There was another rare instant of unsteadiness in a Metropolitan Championship played at Fox Hills, Staten Island. The qualifying round was over the thirty-six-hole route. One very well-known golfer astonished every one by playing the first eighteen holes in 99. Then, to the even greater astonishment of those present, he played the last eighteen in 74. Now here was a difference of twenty-five strokes in two consecutive rounds, played the same day over the same course. It seems impossible that there could be such a wide gap, but golf has known many sudden shifts. In the first round the player not only played bad golf, but everything broke against him. In the second round everything broke his way, and he quickly settled to a steady swing.

These shifts, of course, are almost entirely mental —not physical. There might be a physical difference of three or four strokes, or perhaps five or six. But the difference between playing with confidence and playing in a state of upset nerves might be, as shown above, anywhere from ten to twenty-five strokes a round.

HOODOO HOLES

Most troubles in golf, after one has developed the main principles of a natural swing, are mental, not physical. I once heard a prominent amateur say that he wouldn't miss one shot a year if he could only keep his head still—could only keep from looking up. And he wasn't far from right.

These mental troubles come in various ways. Golfers very often on their home courses have holes that furnish them any amount of trouble, holes not particularly hard, perhaps, but that are associated with missed shots, until they get on the golfer's nerves.

Trouble of this sort is all mental. The golfer, remembering that he has played the hole badly on the round before, becomes over anxious, is too careful, and either jerks his head up or presses his shot. When he has played a hole badly two or three times in succession he makes up his mind the hole is a hoodoo proposition, and so begins to worry about it from the moment he reaches the tee. And very frequently this worry or foreboding, especially in a medal round, will start many holes before the ill-fated one is reached.

Since a matter of this sort is purely mental it must be cured by mental application, and the best way is to school one's self to indifference, to practise the matter of concentration upon each shot, rather than of concentration upon any trouble ahead. These mental lessons, as suggested before, must be practised as well as the physical ones. Since the mental is such a big part of the game, it stands to reason that it must receive its share of consideration.

The point is that one must drill one's self to think about *making*, not *missing*, the shot.

Take, in this respect, the case of the late Fred Tait, one of the greatest golfers that ever lived. Mr. Tait was a wonderful example of concentration upon the next shot ahead, forgetting mistakes behind and trouble that might come. In the final of his last championship at Prestwick, just before his death in the Boer War, he met the redoubtable John Ball. They were neck and neck coming to the well-known Alps, the seventeenth hole. Here Tait, coming up to the green, found that he had played his second shot into a bunker full of water, guarding the green. Without wasting time in crying his ill-luck, the lion-hearted Tait waded in grimly and played as fine a shot as if he had had the most perfect of lies, winning the championship.

There is more to golf than mere shot making. The greatest shot maker in the world may not be the greatest golfer, for golf, in addition to ability to play shots properly, requires mental and physical stamina, poise, concentration, nerve, and the control of the nerves.

There is no such thing for any man as eternal steadiness, but there is no reason why most golfers shouldn't develop a much greater steadiness than is shown. It is all a matter of practising two things—the proper use of the club, and concentration, or nerve control. Remember, at each practice, or during each friendly round, to try and make your brain work as well as your arms and legs. Remember, above all other factors, that it is vital to the success of the shot that you keep your head still—often referred to as "looking at the ball." Make it a point to school your brain as well as your muscles, for the brain is in control of the muscles. The golfer who can't concentrate, who doesn't practise concentration, will never be able to develop steadiness, although he may be a fine shot maker, and may be capable of some wonderful rounds.

So, to put a few suggestions into compact, concrete form, the following are offered to those who desire a

MY FAULT LAY IN THE FACT THAT AS I STARTED MY CLUB
BACK, I BENT MY WRIST TOO FAR, BREAKING THE SWING

change for the better in the golfing steadiness, or un-steadiness:

1. Practise concentration—keeping your *mind* on the ball as well as your eye.

2. Make up your mind to accept a bad lie *or* some bad luck as part of the game and to be expected.

3. Play each shot as it comes, without *regret* over past mistakes *or* worry over future troubles.

4. Practise the short game, shots around the green, at every possible chance. It is here that scores are reduced.

5. Practise with the brain, as well as with the arms and legs. Cultivate brain control over muscle.

THREE UP ON ANANIAS

A group of golfers sat one day
  Around the Nineteenth Hole,
Exchanging lies and alibis
  Athwart the flowing bowl;
" Let's give a cup," said one of them,
  A sparkle in his eye,
" For him among us who can tell
  The most outrageous lie."

" Agreed"—they cried—and one by one
  They played 'er under par,
With yarns of putts and brassie shots
  That travelled true and far;
With stories of prodigious swipes—
  Of holes they made in one—
Of niblick shots from yawning traps
  As Vardon might have done.

And then they noticed, sitting by,
  Apart from all the rest,
A stranger who had yet to join
  The fabricating test;
"Get in the game," they said to him,
  "Come on and shoot your bit"—
Whereat the stranger rose and spoke
  As follows—or to wit:

" Although I've played some holes in one,
  And other holes in two;
Although I've often beaten par,
  I kindly beg of you
To let me off—for while I might
  Show proof of well-earned fame,
I NEVER SPEAK ABOUT MY SCORES—
OR TALK ABOUT MY GAME."

          .   .   .   .   .

They handed him the cup at once,
  Their beaten banners furled;
Inscribing first below his name—
  THE CHAMPION OF THE WORLD.

V

GOLF AND THE FICKLE GODDESS

WHAT part does the Fickle Goddess—
Luck, Fate, Chance, or what you may
care to call her—play in Golf?

According to Walter J. Travis and other experts
luck is only a small part of the game. They point
to the fact that Vardon, Braid, and Taylor are the
three greatest golfers in the world, and that among
them they have won sixteen British Open Championships, showing that merit succeeds above any other
factor.

Merit, or ability, undoubtedly succeeds above any
other factor. But this doesn't mean that blind luck
plays no important part in individual matches.
Good luck has won—and hard luck has lost—more
than one well-played, hard-fought match over the

sweep of the ancient green. In the long run luck may even up, but in an 18-hole or a 36-hole match, luck may be all on one side, or largely enough on one side to decide the issue.

Those who refuse to credit this should ask John G. Anderson. Some years ago Anderson met Chick Evans in the final round for the Amateur Championship of France. For thirty-seven holes these two fought out a brilliant duel of wood and iron without advantage. The second extra hole was a par 4. Evans's tee shot was well below his average, and Anderson had visions of victory at last. Teeing the ball up he took his stance. Just as he reached the top of his swing, and the club head started for the ball, a large touring car swept around the road curve and emitted a series of loud and raucous honks just a few yards behind the player. Under the high, nervous tension Anderson naturally shied, swung wildly, struck the ball high up in the heel of the club, and dispatched it to an unplayable lie back of a tree to the left of the course where he required three shots to play out. He was on the green in 5 and went down in one put, getting a 6. Evans finally had to hole a 10-foot putt for a win in 5.

BLOW FOR EVANS

Fortune favoured Evans that day, but the fickle goddess hasn't always been with the Chicago star. In fact, he has had more than his share of tough breaks. At Ekwanok, in 1914, the Western star drew Eben M. Byers, one of the hardest fighters of the game, in his first round of match play. The two came to the last hole all square. Byers got away a short tee shot that barely cleared the rough. Evans half topped his drive into the long grass in front of the tee.

One hundred and fifty yards beyond this long grass there was a deep ditch to catch a poorly played second shot. Recent rains had left the fairway soft where the ball generally struck with but little run, frequently not travelling over a yard or two, even after a drive. Playing from the heavy grass,

Evans used a light mashie and, attempting to play safely this side of the pitch, pitched at least twenty-five yards short. To the amazement of himself and the big gallery, the ball struck and bounded forward as if landing on stone, winding up in the ditch. This shot put Evans out of the championship, and to this day no one has been able to account for the terrific run of the ball, except that it struck upon a hard plot where 99-100 of the remaining area was soft and sufficiently soggy to have left an easy poke for the green and the certainty of a halved hole.

In the same tournament at Ekwanok Francis Ouimet had a hard match with young Max Marston, who was moving at top speed. They came to the fourteenth tee all even. Just in front of this tee there is a veritable chasm to carry, 30 or 40 feet deep and at least 150 feet wide. A topped shot almost surely means disaster here, for at the bottom there is a flooring of rock and underbrush, leaving an unplayable lie nine times out of ten. Ouimet's shot, badly topped, spun into this cavernous depth. No **one** figured that he had a chance to even get a half, as Marston's long drive sailed within short pitching distance of the green. But when Ouimet descended and found his ball, it was resting nicely in an open spot, and from here he proceeded to play out in one shot, land on the green, go down in one put, and win with a 3 against Marston's par 4. This put him one up, and it was by that narrow margin that he won the match. Granted that the amateur champion made a brilliant, courageous shot; but how often does a golfer find a perfect lie in a cavern replete with rocks and huge boulders and a heavy undergrowth?

Two golfers will top their seconds into a bunker. One will lie nicely, awaiting an easy pitch out to the green. The other will be jam up against the bank or in a heel print in the sand, where there will be at least the difference of a stroke. Breaks in luck of this type occur frequently. There are also breaks where one man's topped shot will stop just short of a trap where another's runs deeply in, making the difference of a stroke or more. Ted Ray, for example, will never forget the sixteenth hole at Sandwich. The par here is 3, and a 4 would have given Ray the championship that year. His tee shot caught the trap, and when he came to the ball, it was not only up against the side of the bunker, but was lying deep in a heel print. Ray is a master of the niblick, and the one he carries is more like a shovel. But even with this doughty weapon he was unable to dislodge the ball, and at his second vain shot he saw the championship pass on beyond. A few minutes later on Harold, with a 3 to win at this hole after Ray had failed, put his tee shot in almost the identical spot and he found lodgement in a heel hole that looked as if some one had blasted out the spot. Hilton, too, was unable to get out, and lost his chance.

In both cases you say this was the result of a poor tee shot and not of hard luck. This is only partly so. Nine times out of ten Ray would have been able to play out from any trap with the loss of only that one stroke. But one poor shot cost him at least two more, which is a heavier penalty than Dame Fortune should ordinarily require.

Perhaps no one has a harder-luck case to cite than Jack Hobens, the Englewood, N. J., professional. One spring Hobens played in the North and South Open Championship at Pinehurst. Over the full route he finished in a tie with Alex. Ross. The play off followed, and nearing the finish Hobens was a stroke to the good. At this point he hooked his tee shot to the edge of the fairway, but the ball was resting where he had an easy iron shot to the sand green. As his club came back the shaft or blade struck a vine somewhere in the rear, and it so happened that this particular vine had an almost invisible creeper attached which rested directly under the ball. The result was that the ball was jostled out of its position, costing one stroke, and Hobens then missed it completely, costing another—for when his club head came in to the ball the aforesaid ball was several inches beyond its original position. This attached creeper cost Hobens the championship, and all through no fault or mistake of his own.

Another Englewood golfer with a legitimate claim to hard luck is Oswald Kirkby, metropolitan champion. In 1911 the Metropolitan Open was put on at his club. Kirkby was then playing brilliant golf, with a good chance to win. He had recorded a round of 69 and was either leading the field at the time or within a stroke of the top. Coming to the twelfth hole he had a chance to break 70 again and take the lead by a safe margin. This hole is only 300 yards long—an almost sure and an easily possible 3, as Kirkby was playing. He hooked his tee shot here, and when he came to the ball found that it had rolled into a crevice in a stone ledge to the left of the course. It was probably the one spot within a radius of 20 yards that would have cost more than one shot. When Kirkby finished he had required 8 strokes and his chance for the championship had passed.

All luck, however, isn't bad luck. When Jamie Anderson was playing in the British Open at St. Andrews one year, he teed his ball and stepped up to play an iron shot for the green. As he was making his preliminary address a small urchin standing by called out, "Hey, Jamie—ye're outside the disks." Anderson looked and saw that the urchin was right. Moving the ball back to its proper location Jamie then proceeded to hole out in one shot. With that break in his favour there could be only one answer: he won the championship.

In a tournament at Apawamis two golfers of fair ability were playing a practice round the day before scheduled proceedings were to begin. Near the finish one of them, swinging a mashie, struck the other's knee and left a deep cut. The injured player was carried into the clubhouse bewailing his hard luck. The next day, limping badly, he entered the tournament just to get in a round of golf more than anything else. At the start he was still complaining of the hard blow Fate had struck him. To his great surprise and the surprise of others he not only qualified in a higher flight than he had ever figured on, but he emerged the winner of this flight with several of the best rounds he had ever played. The answer is that his supposedly hard luck had been good luck. After his accident he was forced to take an easy swing, he had no chance to press, and as a result he kept straight down the course. He had to play safe rather than take a chance on any long shot, and so through the margin of an injured knee he did better than he had ever done in his golfing career.

In the main most golfers will find that luck pretty well evens up. The trouble is that the golfer will remember bitterly the putt that hit the cup and jumped out, or the bad lie which cost a shot, forgetting the topped mashie that ran dead to the hole or the topped brassie that jumped through a bunker and bounded merrily upon the green. He will remember the short four-footer that rimmed the cup but will make no mention of the thirty-footer that dropped in with a resounding cluck and saved from one to three strokes. He will remember the long carry that just caught the trap, forgetting the poorly played blow that just stopped short of trouble.

There is plenty of luck in golf, good luck and bad luck, but the winning golfer is the one who takes both as they come, all as a part of the game.

DOUBLE-CROSSING TRADITION

*(The best showing made by an American amateur of
late years was by Heinrich Schmidt at St. Andrews.)*

*When a Schmidt at St. Andrews can beat a Mac-
    Phearson*
    And beat him a good city block;
When a Heinie can bandy a cleek with a Sandy
    And finish two up on a Jock;
When the swirl of the kilts at the top o' the swipe
    Finds a German is nearer the plat,
What is left in the name or the slant of a game
    That can stand for a sputter like that,
            Aye, mon,
    That can stand for a sputter like that?

When the home of the stymie, the green, and the putter
    Finds Rabbie and Jock by the tee,

THE WINNING SHOT

Gazing wildly at chronic approaches Teutonic
    That trickle up dead for a "three"—
When it's aye doonricht certain that Scotia's curtain
    Must yield to a Heinrich or such,
Where's the future in store that can heal up the sore
    Of a stymie set up by the Dutch,
            Hoot, mon,
Of a stymie set up by the Dutch?

VI

HEROES OF WOOD AND IRON

NEARLY every golfer has his favourite club. With some this club is a driver; with others a mid-iron or a mashie; with still others it is the putter.

Any number of plain, ordinary average golfers, far from the championship lists, are masters with one club. Any number of these average golfers, who are wonders at pitching a mashie shot close to the hole, are badly defective in their driving and long iron play. Any number of golfers who rarely play below eighty-eight or ninety are better putters than many stars.

In practically all other games there is but one club to use. In golf there are from five to ten clubs in use, and at least five distinct shots—the drive, the full iron, the mashie pitch, the chip shot, and the putt.

Each is played differently and requires a particular kind of skill.   So an average golfer may be good with one certain club and poor with another.   There are clubs in the bag which a golfer takes out with great confidence, and others which he takes out with great fear and reluctance, although the latter may be easier clubs for most to use than the former.   All of which is a part of the mystery of the game.

APPLIES TO STARS AS WELL

This liking for a certain club or for certain clubs, and distrust for other clubs, isn't confined to the duffer or to the average golfer.   It applies as well to the great stars of the game—to the Vardons, the Hiltons, the Ouimets, the Taylors, and the Braids.

Take the case of Francis Ouimet, American Open Champion for 1913 and Amateur Champion for 1914. Ouimet, to my mind, is the soundest of all American amateurs when every club in the bag is to be considered.   He is no better than Evans from the tee up to the green, but he is a far better putter.

Yet if I had to pick out one club with which Ouimet is best, I should say the driver. He is a fine wooden-club player, especially on brassie shots from fairly close lies, the supreme test of wooden-club play. When he beat Vardon and Ray at Brookline he was as accurate with the wood as Vardon, and almost as long as the mighty Ray.

A OUIMET SHOT

In the Amateur Championship, held at Ekwanok, Ouimet and W. C. Fownes had one of the hardest matches of the week. Fownes was one up at the thirty-fourth hole but lost the thirty-fifth, bringing them to the last hole all square. This hole, about 450 yards, played as it was against the wind, with the course soft, calls for two fine shots to make the green. Both got away good drives, but Fownes was unable to get home on his second.

I saw Ouimet walk up to his ball and study the lie and the distance. He had a close lie that ordinarily would have called for an iron shot. If he topped with his brassie there was a deep ditch ahead that meant disaster. But he reached for the wood, and as he did so I turned to a friend and remarked, "That ends the match; he'll put this on the green sure." I knew what he could do with that wooden club. The result was a wonderful shot, 220 yards from a close lie against the wind plump into the middle of the green for a sure four and the match. If he hadn't been a master of the wood he would never have got on, and Fownes might have beaten him later on.

THE CASE OF HILTON

Harold Hilton, the great English amateur, is a finely rounded golfer, but I should say his two favourite shots are the spoon and the chip shot. It is my belief that from sixty yards up to the green, Hilton goes down in two oftener than any other golfer in the world. Not that he is such a wonderful putter, but largely because he nearly always lands that chip shot within easy putting distance.

Hilton is almost as accurate with a spoon, a

wooden club for closer lies and shorter distances than the brassie calls for. In his match at Sandwich against Harris in the British Amateur, Hilton came to a shot which called for a 200-yard distance, with a strong following wind. He could have reached the green easily with a mid-iron. I would never have thought of using any other club. To my surprise he took out his spoon and played with an easy swing, placing the ball within eight feet of the hole and then sinking his putt. It was a ticklish shot, and so he went to the club in which he had greatest confidence. Yet nine golfers out of ten would have found the mid-iron much the easiest and much the safest club to use at that point.

JOHN BALL AND THE MID-IRON

John Ball, eight times British Amateur Champion, who won his first championship in 1888 and his last one in 1912, twenty-four years apart, like Hilton, is a master of nearly every club in the bag.

But Ball can do tricks with a mid-iron that no

other golfer would ever think of doing. He lives at Hoylake, and very frequently goes out for a round with nothing but a mid-iron. A big part of the time he doesn't even take a mashie along—the one club considered the most necessary of all clubs in the bag.

Just before the British Amateur Championship, in 1913, Ball was standing in a bunker playing shots from a deep trap where most golfers would have been thankful to get out with a niblick. Ball was using a mid-iron. Shot after shot he laid up within putting distance of the cup. It looked to be so easy that a certain golfer, one of the best, figured that he could, also, make the shot. "Here, let me take a crack at it," he said to Ball. Ball smiled and handed the mid-iron over. The golfer descended into the trap, waled away, and came near losing an eye. The ball struck the side of the trap and came back so swiftly that one of the experimenter's optics was closed.

In a hard match at Hoylake, Ball came to the fourteenth hole, where the second shot frequently catches a heavy patching of whins short of the green. Ball's second landed in these whins and he had a tough lie. I expected to see him take a niblick, and was wondering whether he could even get out with this club. But he again reached for his mid-iron, and not only played the ball out, but with such terrific back spin that it carried low and still pulled up as if it had been pitched with a mashie-niblick.

AN AMERICAN MARVEL

One of the most pronounced instances of supremacy with one club is that of Jesse Guilford, the New Hampshire player. Although a good golfer, he was hardly known beyond the borders of his native state until the Amateur Championship at Ekwanok. Here, within a few days, he was one of the sensations of the tournament, and largely through the terrific distance he was able to get with his driver.

Guilford is a powerfully built young fellow, weighing about one hundred and ninety pounds, but he was figured as a young country boy who knew little about the game. But those looking for an easy match were given another guess when they saw him hit a few from the tee. Using a swing that came back to his left heel, and crashing in with fine timing and terrific force, Guilford was from fifteen to thirty yards farther than Kirkby, Herreshoff, and others regarded as the longest hitters in the game. Ouimet drives a long ball, but he couldn't get within twenty-five yards of Guilford. On one occasion, when Guilford hit one that looked as if it would never land, the distance of the carry alone was measured and found to be 312 yards! A carry of 200 yards or 220 yards is supposed to be a long one.

On holes of 450 yards, where his opponent was using a drive and a full brassie, Guilford was easily home with a drive and a mashie. Once he drove into the ditch at the eighteenth hole, put there to catch the second shot—and this ditch is fully 330 yards from the tee, if not a bit longer. All this with the ground soft from recent rains.

How did he get all this distance? Simply by fine

timing, great physical strength, and an overswing that few golfers could control. If the average good player swung at a golf ball as Guilford does, he would be lucky to get two shots in ten anywhere near the center of the course. Guilford's swing is absolutely free without a cultivated touch.

THE STAR TRAVIS SHOT

Walter J. Travis, the American veteran, has always been an accurate player. And yet but for one club he has lacked the distance, both with wood and iron, to reach championship heights.

This one club that has saved Travis is the putter, and especially when he uses it for an approach putt. I don't believe any other man that ever played has laid as many long approach putts dead to the hole. This applies not only on the green, but off the green, where most golfers would use a jigger, a mid-iron, or a mashie. But if the surface is fairly smooth Travis is sure to reach for his putter, although five or ten yards from the edge of the green, and he is almost as sure to place the ball within easy putting distance if he doesn't lay it absolutely dead.

It was with this shot, in the main, that Travis won the British Amateur Championship. Although in place of laying these long approaches dead he was holing a big share of them, going down in one from distances where Blackwell, his opponent, was fighting to get down in two.

It is almost uncanny to watch Travis on a putt thirty feet away, and see how close to the cup his shot invariably stops, leaving him practically nothing to do on his next shot, which often is the most nerve-racking of them all—the putts of three and four feet.

VARDON AND EVANS

In many ways the play of Vardon and Evans remind me more of each other than any other two in the game. Both are fine off the tee. Vardon's best shot is a full iron to the green and close to the pin, and this, too, I consider the best shot Evans carries. Once on the green, both are poor putters; but Vardon is a better putter than Evans, for there are many occasions when Vardon putts unusually well. It is only in comparison with the rest of the game that his putting looks bad. If these players were fine putters they would never be beaten, except by each other.

DISPELLING A MYSTERY

It might be just as well here to dispel some of the mystery which many golfers carry in regard to wood and iron play.

Off the tee, the golfer has a full, free swipe at the ball. There is no restriction as to distance. He can hit it as hard as he likes, his main object being to keep the ball straight down the course. In this shot there is no need of any muscular control. It is merely a matter of having the right swing and keeping the head still.

But take a shot of 140 yards; here the element of control enters; here the golfer must have a grip upon his strength. If he hits a straight shot 160 yards, he will be well over the green into some deep trap. If he hits a straight shot 120 yards, he will drop short of the green into some deep trap. He must not only be straight, but he must hit that ball just 140 yards, or in that immediate neighbourhood. Some golfers who haven't the free swing or the snap to drive 200 yards still have the nerve and muscular control necessary to play these short-distance shots accurately. Others who can drive 250 yards, where there is no restraint to be placed upon their shots, lack the control to handle a club for a restricted shot.

The chief fault generally in this latter respect is overswinging. A golfer who swings a mashie high up around his neck has no chance to compete in control with the golfer who comes only three quarters of the way back. And yet I should say that three golfers out of four, at least, swing entirely too far back on all iron shots. Yet they are surprised because they are unable to control a swing that would baffle a Vardon or a Braid. If they would only practise a shorter swing with the mashie or jigger, they would soon be surprised to see how quickly their game improved.

But no man can control a 140-yard shot with a swing that should drive a ball 200 yards.

THE FREAK SHOT

Once in a while, of course, by starting early and by constant practice a man may develop a freak shot with some club that few others could play. There is the case of H. D. Gillies, the great English amateur. When I first saw him play I thought he had a grave fault in pitching his mashie shots too high, hitting them from 120 yards away as if he intended to drive 190. The ball would then travel high into the air, almost twice as high as an average mashie shot. It seemed impossible that any one could control this shot. Yet I soon found that Gillies had it mastered, and that he was as close to the pin as the best.

Gillies could never have mastered this shot if he hadn't taken up the game very young, and perfected it while his muscles were still supple and easy to control.

There is another golfer, a state champion, who

holds his hands six inches apart with every club. This violates every law of proper gripping. Yet by starting this freak grip while young he soon got the hang of it, made it natural, and now is a very steady player, although not so brilliant a one as he would have been had he spent the same amount of time and practice on a surer, simpler grip.

THE BEST WORK OF TAYLOR

It is queer how often a man is supposed to be at his best with one club, whereas the best part of his game may lie in another direction. I know in my own case that I am supposed to be better with the jigger than anything else, when I feel confident that, barring the putter, I have saved more matches with full iron shots from 200 yards or more away.

I had always heard that J. H. Taylor, five times British Open Champion, was ordinary off the tee, but did his greatest work with the mashie. On my last trip over, Fred Herreshoff and I played with Taylor one day at Suningdale. And of all the great driving

I have ever seen, Taylor that day gave a real exhibition. He was not so long as Braid, Ray, or Vardon, but he was long enough, and every tee shot was as accurately placed as if he walked down and dropped the ball with his hand. It was almost beyond belief. His direction was not a matter of yards, but of feet and inches. I commented on this that night, and two English golf reporters who happened to be around then said that Taylor's best work was off the tee, just where he was supposed to be weakest. They mentioned the fact that his control with the wood was especially valuable in tournament play on windy or rainy days, where he still maintained his deadly accuracy down the course.

BRAID'S PLAY

Vardon, Taylor, and Braid are the Big Three of golf. Braid is a very fine wooden-club player, not as accurate as Vardon or Taylor, but above the average. But Braid, I should say, was the weakest of the three in iron play—and the best putter of the lot. In fact,

I should say he is the best putter among the professionals abroad. With wood and iron play that would have meant sure defeat to Vardon, Braid has been able to win championships with his exceptional putting. In addition to which he is a rare fighter, and this, too, has been a big factor in his success.

THE CLASH OF IRONS

The most spectacular feature of any tournament comes when two fine iron players meet. This was proved in the great match at Ekwanok for the Amateur Championship between Chick Evans and Eben Byers. Byers that day was driving poorly, but was playing his iron shots finely and putting brilliantly. Evans was driving brilliantly, playing his irons well, and putting badly. Byers's bad driving was offset by Evans's poor putting, turning the match into a battle of the irons.

When they came to the twelfth tee Byers was one up. This hole is about 340 yards, with the green over a hill and well tapped, a green hard to approach

[136]

and hold. Byers's drive was far off in the rough. Evans was straight down the course. From the high grass, 150 yards away, Byers brought applause from the gallery by playing his mashie to within two feet of the cup. It was a wonderful shot, and Evans looked to be beaten. But the applause for Byers soon broke into a roar, when Evans, from 140 yards away, laid his mashie shot within four inches of the cup, leaving two white balls nestled right at the hole. But Byers missed his short putt and the match was all even. He made up for this, however, by laying a 160-yard shot at the fifteenth hole up within two feet of the cup, winning the hole, and finally winning the match by this margin.

No matter how wonderfully a man may be driving, if he is off with his irons or is putting poorly, he has but little chance. A good long putt may save many a poor drive or bad iron shot, but a missed short putt spoils the best drive ever made.

Probably no man who ever won a championship has had as much trouble with the wood as I have.

The queer part of it is that, after missing wooden-club shots, I can pick up a driving iron and get both distance and direction. But in this way I believe that frequently being off with one club has a tendency to improve a man's play with another. It drives him into a desperation that often seems to produce results. After missing a tee shot I know then, in my own case, that I can't afford to make any more mistakes, and so in a way get more careful and take a harder grip upon myself. When a man doesn't get a chance to loaf in a tight match he loses that feeling of over-confidence, and when he recovers from a bad position the psychological effect is all his way.

HARDEST AND EASIEST SHOTS

I have heard many debates as to the hardest and the easiest clubs to play. I should say the hardest shot in the game, the one that has fewer masters, is the full iron shot to the green. Running a close second is the mashie pitch. There are fewer golfers by far who can play these two shots well than those who are good drivers or good putters. The easiest shot in golf is the drive, and the simplest is the putt. But as putting is almost purely a mental proposition, it probably varies more with all players than any other shot.

You see very few good sound iron players, especially among the amateurs in America. In England their iron play is much better. The main difference between the professionals and the amateurs is all in iron play. There are amateurs who can putt better than the best professionals. There are many who can drive as well. But there are, in America, only two or three who can play an iron up to the professional standard.

It is hard to explain just why certain clubs appeal so strongly to certain players. In much the same way a baseball player becomes attached to a certain bat. It may not suit another player, but it has exactly the right feeling for him.

Here and there the golfer runs across a club with a perfect balance. When he gets a club of that type money could hardly buy it. In England, on my last trip, I happened to pick up a certain light iron in a professional's shop. It was rusty and several years old. Yet I knew the minute I got my hands on that club it was exactly what I wanted. The professional was glad to sell an old club cheap. So I bought it for a dollar. The next day Fred Herreshoff picked it up, and offered me five dollars for my bargain. I refused, and he offered me ten dollars. He finally offered twenty-five dollars, but I told him it was not for sale.

Some years ago "Snake" Ames, the old Princeton football star, who is also a fine golfer, had a mashie in his bag which he rarely used. One day he handed it to Oswald Kirkby, who had been looking for a mashie that suited him. "It's exactly the club I've been looking for," said Kirkby. "Please keep it then," said Ames, "I've been looking for a chance to get rid of it."

Within a week two golfers offered Kirkby thirty dollars for the club, but fifty dollars would not have

MORE BAD SHOTS ARE MADE FROM "LOOKING UP"—NOT LOOKI
THE BALL—THAN ANY OTHER ONE FACTOR

tempted him. And any new mashie on the market can be bought for three dollars. The feel and balance of this club merely happened to have an appeal to several players beyond that of any other mashie they had ever used. Yet to its original owner it was worthless. This club is now Kirkby's prize possession, and it isn't for sale at any price.

When a man gets a club of this sort, whether it be driver, brassie, iron, or putter, he is almost sure to play it well. For a big part of golf is confidence. If a golfer believes he can make a certain shot, he can generally make it. If he has unusual confidence in a certain club, he is almost sure to use it well; and in every hard match he is equally sure to use it at every chance, even when at times the shot would naturally call for a different sort of club.

RAY'S PET CLUB

Edward Ray, ex-British champion, has a massive niblick that he uses for every pitch shot from 150 to 50 yards. Where the average golfer would take a full mashie or perhaps a jigger, Ray takes out this niblick for a high pitch that is almost sure to fall dead.

At Baltusrol, in his match with Vardon against two American stars, he played a shot with this club that is still the talk of the big gallery which followed the contest.

Coming to the sixth hole he hooked his shot behind a solid fringe of tall trees. There was absolutely no way to play through these trees to the green. And he was so close in that it seemed impossible that he could pitch over them. But calling for the spade-like niblick he shot the ball almost directly straight up from the turf, barely arching it over the trees and on to the green, within four feet of the hole, where he got a three, beating par by a stroke from a lie that hardly another golfer could have played at all. He simply had abounding confidence in this club, such confidence that he believed any miracle was possible with it.

A ROUND OF THE COURSE

OR, THE RECREATIVE ADVANTAGES OF GOLF FOR THE TIRED BUSINESS MAN

Worn out, depressed and melancholy,
A victim of hard labour's folly,
With nerves awry and out of gear,
With sodden heart bereft of cheer,
I sought, beyond the toiling scene,
The solace of the ancient green.

I needed rest and recreation,
To foster mental elevation,
Something to lift my morbid soul
From out its sordid daily rôle,
To give my frazzled nerves a rest
From troubles that harassed my breast.

THE WINNING SHOT

And so, with joyous buoyant mind,
I left all work and care behind
And beat it to the swarded plot
Of soaring drive and mashie shot.
I hit my opening drive a bang.
" This is the life!" my gay heart sang.

FIRST HOLE

A noble shot—a lusty clout—
   In fact, a most amazing rap;
And then I took my mashie out,
   To pitch beyond the guarding trap.
Did I look up just as I hit?
   Or did I shift my wrist or knee?
My topped ball fluttered to the pit
   And something died inside of me.

SECOND HOLE

I teed one up to let it ride,
   To make up for that other miss;
The doggone pill sailed furlongs wide
   And dropped into a deep abyss.

[144]

A ROUND OF THE COURSE

It took me eight before I got
    The ball at last into the hole,
And though my niblick blade was hot,
    'Twas not as sultry as my soul.

THIRD HOLE

A corking drive—a mashie pitch
    That sailed upon its way serene,
That cleared each guarding trap and ditch
    And landed lightly on the green.
My sagging heart forgot its blight—
    Forgotten now each bitter curse;
And then, with easy par in sight,
    I took four putts and felt still worse.

FOURTH HOLE

I soaked the next one straight and true,
    And then—oh, ancient alibi!—
I bade all joy a last adieu—
    My ball had found a cuppy lie!

[145]

THE WINNING SHOT

I tore my hair and wept aloud,

When I had flubbed, depressed and sore;

And then, a blighted wretch and cowed,

I marked eight more against my score.

THE OTHER FOURTEEN

I made my way from bad to worse;

I sliced and foozled, hooked and topped

Until at last, with bitter curse,

Upon the final green I flopped.

And writhing there, a broken thing,

My stark soul echoed one last cry—

"Oh, Death, where is thy bitter sting?

Oh, Grave, where is thy victory?"

And this we label sport and fun,

When other grinding work is done!

And this we go to with a zest,

For recreation and a rest

"Tired business man"—a phrase inspired!

My word! No wonder he is tired!

A BYRONIC APPEAL

Game of golluf, heed this pote—
Give, Oh, give me back my goat.

Once I knew no care or sigh;
Now I rave within my sleep;
Once I could not tell a lie;
Now I make my caddie weep;
Once I knew no alibi;
Now there's nothing else I keep.

Once I never grew profane;
Now I simply let 'er rip;
Once I had a useful brain,
Actively upon the flip;
Now I waste my time in vain
Grappling with the Vardon grip.

THE WINNING SHOT

Once Ambition was astir
To succeed at trade—or books;
Now I dabble in a whirr
Of elusive "tops" and "hooks";
Once I gave my life to Her—
Now I wonder how she looks.

Once I used to work a while;
Now I never see the store;
Once I could have made a pile;
Now I only make a score;
Once my presence meant a smile—
Now I am an Awful Bore.

Game of golluf, heed this pote—
Give, Oh, give me back my goat.

VII

VARDON—GREATEST GOLFER

IF YOU should ever visit the British Isles while a big golf tournament is in progress and should desire to watch Harry Vardon, with no one around to point Vardon out, I can furnish you at least one simple direction that will make the quest easy:

You will hardly discover him off the tee where there will be many far and straight.

You will hardly be able to pick him out within one hundred and fifty yards of the hole where there will be many near the pin on their next shot.

But when, out of the big field, you run across one man who is making the game look so easy that a child might play it, whose form is the last word in poetry, and who from one hundred and eighty to two hundred and twenty yards is putting a full shot closer to the pin than most cracks can place a mashie, you may know that at last you are looking at the greatest golfer the world has ever seen—and your quest for Vardon will be over.

Some wise sport philosopher has said: "When a race is run truly, the best is always first at the finish." The championship of golf has been truly run then, for it is exactly fitting that of the sixteen open championships won by Britain's great triumvirate, Vardon should have won six, Braid five, and Taylor five, leaving the two latter only a short length back of the master workman.

To my mind an intimate study of the golfing methods of Vardon, Braid, and Taylor, the Big Three, is the most interesting study connected with golf; not only because these three lead the field, but because they have reached the top over three separate trails of form and style.

There are other great golfers in the world, notably Ted Ray and George Duncan among others, but when all is said and written there can be no question that Vardon, Braid, and Taylor, with their sixteen world championships out of twenty years' play, are at present far in the front.

THE BIG THREE

It has been my pleasure to have played with James Braid and J. H. Taylor over their own native soil, and to have watched Vardon play in championship tests. And of my entire experience at golf, nothing has been so interesting to me as to make comparisons at close range of these three wizards.

There can be no question that of them all Vardon is the nonpareil of the game, greater for a number of reasons, but largely because he has better control over a greater number of great shots. Of all golfers, his form is the most beautiful, the most rhythmic, the most perfect—to borrow a phrase out of joint. From that day, eighteen years ago, when at the age of twenty-six he stepped out and won his first British blue ribbon, the golfing world knew that a master had come. For here was a golfer whose foundation was too sound to be rocked. His mental equipment was flawless. His disposition was even, unbroken, and placid—placid but not flabby. He had the ideal soul for the game, a soul that took each break of the game as it came to him without a quiver or a complaint.

But even above all that, his mastery of a golf ball was complete. Playing with the old gutty ball, he could almost make it sit up and dance, eat out of his hand, with any club in the bag. It wasn't until the new lively ball came in and began to elude the cup from his putter that Vardon found a rival. Even then he had control of the ball from the tee up to the green, and only his putting prevented him from winning twelve championships in place of only six.

VARDON'S STYLE

I am not going into any technical explanation or description of all that Vardon does—of his style complete. But there are several important details worth pointing out. In driving, Vardon makes the shot look absolutely simple. He has a free, easy swing, and while he gets good distance, he never makes any attempt to get all the distance possible.

If you will notice most of the star golfers' driving in this country, you will see that they play with a round, flat swing that is inclined to produce a hooked ball. Vardon, on the contrary, employs an upright swing, in which he keeps the club head within the intended line of flight as long as possible. His is more of a pendulum affair, in which the timing is miraculously true. The timing of all Vardon's shots is truer than that of any other player, which can only be explained by saying that he was born with a championship knack and developed it, and held it by constant work and practice.

Another point: Vardon, in place of bending his left knee well in toward the right at the top of his swing, bends it a trifle more to the front and just enough to brace himself and to develop perfect poise.

In other words, Vardon seems to play each stroke

the easiest and the simplest way, which is the answer to perfect form. He takes the short cut. "The game is hard enough," he says, "without making it any harder."

HIS BEST SHOT

But wherein, you may ask, is Vardon greater than Braid or Taylor, who are only one championship behind him? Vardon is longer than Taylor from the tee and a trifle steadier than Braid; but I should say the one feature in which Vardon excelled all others was in laying his full shots close to the pin.

There are a number of golfers who from one hundred and forty to one hundred and sixty yards away are likely to lay a mashie shot or a half mid-iron close. But in the full shots Vardon alone is likely to keep on putting his second shot within eight or ten feet. Two hundred and twenty yards from the green the rest are content merely to get on the green with a brassie smash. But Vardon is always shooting for the cup, and with cleek or brassie you will find him on hole after hole up there close enough for a putt—the sole part of the game where he must bow not only to Braid and Taylor, but also to many others.

Except with the putter there seems to be no shot in golf beyond Vardon's magic. I will explain, with one striking example, just what I mean. In one of his championship battles he had come to the seventeenth hole at a tie, with one of his rivals for the top. His drive here travelled a trifle farther than he had calculated, and found a deep rut in a road crossing the course. His opponent, playing first, was nicely on the green in two for a sure four. It seemed that Vardon was beaten to a certainty. His ball was six inches below the top of the ground, in a deep, narrow rut, and the green was one hundred and forty yards away. Vardon took out a heavy niblick, and in place of playing to one side to be sure and get out, took his stance in the direction of the pin and brought the club down with terrific force. To the wonder of the big gallery the ball rose almost straight in the air, and then, with the forward spin imparted, sailed on to within ten feet of the cup. The other man got his four, but Vardon got his three, winning a match that had been practically lost.

With a mashie Vardon can not only put on a back spin that will hold the ball where it lands, but he has shown that he can impart such a big cut that it will hit and bound backward.

FOILED AT LAST

When Vardon won his first championship at Muirfield, those who saw the perfection of his form and the poise of his golfing temperament figured that at last a man had come who would rule the game for years. And so it seemed for the next few seasons. Then came one of the queer and sudden shifts which help give sport its lure. The old gutta-percha ball passed out, making way for the rubber core, a ball much livelier than the old make. Off the tee Vardon controlled this new ball as well as ever. He remained just as deadly upon his approaches, where delicate work is required. But, to the general amazement of the golfing world and to his own disgust, it simply wrecked his putting. I can only explain this in the thought that he early lost confidence on the greens, and it never came back. For ten years he struggled with the putter, playing wonderful golf up to within thirty feet of the hole, only to drop championship after championship by abnormal weakness here. He lost one championship by missing a ten-inch putt. He was as helpless as a child, and it is only quite recently that he has begun to get back at least some of his old-time confidence.

In my opinion, if Vardon had retained his putting skill he would have won twelve championships. His putting improved this last year, and he immediately stepped out in front again for his sixth victory. To show plainly what this loss of his putting confidence meant, some one figured up in the American Open of 1913 that Vardon missed, in the seventy-two-holes play, twelve putts that were fairly easy to make, while Ouimet sank twelve putts of the most daring and difficult type.

There are three details that have put Vardon in the front rank—the leader of them all. I will enumerate them in order:

1. He has the easiest, surest form of any golfer alive, the result of being born into a perfect swing.

2. He has a wonderful temperament for the game, an even, steady poise that is never ruffled or upset, no matter how badly the break goes against him. He has learned the rare art of taking the game just as it comes, with never a complaint.

3. He has had the advantage of keen competition over the most wonderful courses in the world, an advantage no American golfer possesses—and unlike most professionals he practises at every chance. Vardon will work for hours with one club, not so much to improve his play—which could hardly be bettered—but to retain his skill and to make each stroke machine-like, to establish force of habit to such an extent that the club will almost play itself.

Vardon has genius, and with it, a rare combination, the capacity for infinite patience.

After Vardon in golfdom, J. H. Taylor and James Braid come neck and neck. Each has won five World Championships, so there can be little choice. I had the pleasure of playing with Taylor over his home course, Mid-Surrey.

Taylor, unlike Vardon or Braid, is a trifle short and thickset. He weighs fully two hundred pounds. He has a tremendous chest and broad shoulders. And, unlike Vardon and Braid, he makes no attempt to use the full swing in driving. He has proven, for the satisfaction of those who are physically unable to employ a full, free swing, that the half swing can be just as effective.

TAYLOR OF THE MID-SURREY

I had always heard that Taylor was a wizard with the mashie and a very fine putter. In my round with him I found that this was true, but at the finish the thing that impressed me most about his game was his supposedly weakest point—his driving.

English courses, or most of them, are so trapped

and bunkered that it is often necessary—not to drive straight down the middle, but to place the tee shot within a certain narrow limit, to the right or the left. By placing this shot exactly right the hole is opened up for a fairly easy second. In playing with Taylor I noticed after every tee shot that his ball would stop almost exactly at the spot where he would have walked up and placed it with his hand, if he had been permitted. With that short half swing, he is the most accurate driver that I have ever seen. It was not with him a question of yards, but of feet—I might almost say, inches. He was not nearly so long as Vardon or Braid; but no golfer that ever lived is as accurate when Taylor happens to be in the proper mood.

Here again he differed from Vardon and Braid. Their mental state seemed to be always the same, while Taylor was a golfer of moods. He is much more inclined to worry about himself and his game. If he gets off he is likely to be badly off and his game will vary much more than Vardon's will.

In 1913, knowing his own accuracy, he was praying for a windy, rainy campaign. The wind and the rain came, and Taylor started with wonderful confidence and won his fifth championship.

This last year, by wonderful golf, he led Vardon for the first fifty-four holes. Then at the finish, when a fairly easy seventy-eight would have won for him, he suddenly developed the wrong mood, went badly off his game, and took an eighty-three.

This same state of mind, or varying states of mind, showed the day I played with him. In the morning he went at a marvellous clip—getting a sixty-eight. He was absolutely unbeatable by any man. In the afternoon he started badly, began to bother, and played some twelve or fourteen strokes worse.

In the 1913 tournament I spoke of above, played at Holyoke in a wind and rain storm, Taylor, as I mentioned, started in one of his confident moods. And while conditions were ghastly—so bad that even great golfers were playing many shots far out of line—Taylor in that seventy-two holes, requiring over three hundred shots, played but one ball off the course into the rough—one ball out of three hundred under conditions that made it almost impossible to keep the line, with a blinding rain beating down and a young hurricane blowing at shifting angles over the plain.

Another evidence of Taylor's wonderful genius came in the 1914 championship. In the first morning round he played wonderful golf and scored a seventy-four, but one stroke back of Vardon. But in the afternoon his play fell badly back—he was wild and erratic, and was trapped time and again. The average good golfer under these same conditions would have been very lucky to have gotten an eighty-eight. But by the genius of his recoveries, and his wonderful and tremendous determination, he actually finished with a seventy-eight, but four strokes worse than a score gained by almost flawless golf.

One example of his miraculous recoveries came at the tenth hole—a very difficult four. Taylor, having played the first nine badly, started his hole by being bunkered from the tee. He was not only bunkered but badly bunkered, lying fairly close to the wall of the trap. It was a matter of gossip among spectators as to whether he could get out well enough with his niblick to reach the green in three. Imagine their surprise then when he decided to use a spoon. And imagine their wonder when, by slicing the shot out with wonderful carrying power, he not only got out safely, but landed on the green and narrowly missed getting a three.

Taylor's mighty determination, once he gets into a fighting mood, is surpassed by no man in the game—but when one is at times forced to keep up this endless fighting he is at a big disadvantage playing against one like Vardon, who is working easily. This accounts for Taylor's downfall in the last round, when Vardon caught him and passed on to additional glory

—Taylor finally cracking under the heavy strain of making brilliant recoveries.

BRAID OF THE IRON HEART

Over a seventy-two-hole route I would back Vardon against any golfer that has ever lived. But if Vardon and Braid should tie, and the contest should be decided over an eighteen-hole battle, I would pick Braid.

Braid isn't as steady as either Vardon or Taylor, but he is more spectacular than either. When pressed or driven into a corner, I believe he can make shots that no other could ever hope to make, for he has not only a wonderful nerve, but a wonderful physique that enables him to achieve the almost impossible.

Braid to me as a golfer is the most interesting study of them all. I played a thirty-six hole match with him at his own course, Walton Heath, and had the opportunity to study him at close range.

When Braid first swung into professional competition, unlike Vardon and Taylor, he showed little prospect of championship form. He was a poor driver, a very short one from the tee, and a poor putter. But here the dogged determination and iron will of the man entered. He took a putter, and for weeks and months practised for hours at a time until he had mastered this weakness, trying out every possible scheme, studying each effect, until he had found the grip, stances, and general position that felt most natural and produced the best results.

Then he began to practise driving—working, working, week in and week out, until one morning, to his own amazement, he found himself driving a longer ball than he had dreamed of, with forty yards added overnight. He says now that he hasn't any idea as to how this added distance came; but it was hard work that turned the trick.

Off the tee Braid has a fuller swing than Vardon, a mighty swipe, without the body roll of Ted Ray, who is the longest driver in the world.

In my match with Braid I had a good chance to see how brilliantly he could recover. I was playing better that day than I expected to play, and the battle was all even. Coming to one long, hard hole Braid got a fairly short drive. It was hard to reach this green in two even with a good drive. There was a deep bunker just this side of the green, and I expected, of course, to see Braid play short and get on in three. In place of that, using a brassie, he took a mighty wallop, and not only reached the green but passed over it. After a long drive I barely reached the edge in two. We went to Braid's ball and found it in a deep rut back of the green, the hardest sort of shot to play on to a fast, downhill surface. Using a niblick and playing the shot firmly, but delicately, he not only got the ball out, but put enough spin to hold it within twelve feet of the cup. And then he ran down his putt for a four, and after having the hole apparently won easily, I had a hard fight on to get a half.

But after all, you may ask, what is the one thing, the essential thing, the different thing, that lifts these three golfers, especially Vardon, so far above the rest? Above such brilliant players as George Duncan and Ted Ray, above the best America has to offer?

The answer is easy enough: there are fifty golfers who have brilliance; there are only three who have both brilliance and steadiness. They are geniuses —and they are pluggers. They travel at a fast clip, but nearly always at the same clip. There are many golfers who might beat Vardon in an eighteen-hole match. There is none living that could beat him the majority of fifty matches.

At Brookline Ouimet tied with him over seventy-two holes and beat him at eighteen. But at Prestwich Vardon finished first and Ouimet fifty-fifth. It isn't what we can do one day—many of us can play like marvels for a day—but what we can do every day. In England last season he played a re-markable long series of matches—fully a hundred (including championship and matches for big purses over championship courses). *His average score for the entire summer was seventy-four—or almost exactly par golf.* Braid was about seventy-five and Taylor about the same. But the main difference was that Braid and Taylor were often more brilliant—and often a good bit worse—while Vardon has held the even, steady way with less variation than any rival.

Take his trip across America: with Ray as a partner, these two played in something like sixty matches. They lost just one. They travelled over a strange country to strange courses; they put in most of their time on sleepers, where their rest was broken; conditions were badly against them—and yet day in and day out Vardon held the same brilliant, steady pace, breaking a course record one day, playing par golf the next, but always holding his game under perfect control.

By that I mean that if you follow Vardon, Braid, and Taylor in a series of matches, you will notice one thing: it isn't so much the wonder shots of the game which make them great as their strict adherence to the simple but essential things.

That is, you never catch one of them jerking his head up before hitting the ball. "Keep your eye on the ball" is a motto they follow to a finish. Sometimes the rest of us do; sometimes we don't.

"Don't press" is another slogan of the game, and a simple one. The one thing that will impress you about the game of these three is that they are always playing with a lot in reserve. Apparently they are never going the limit in any shot.

There are a lot of good golfers who have perfect grips, perfect stances, and swing in the correct way. But at times under stress or strain they can't help looking up too soon, or swaying the body, or committing some other fault.

But they take care of the main and simpler ingredients of the game—the part where the average golfer falls down.

Most of the shots missed in golf are not missed through a wrong grip, or a bad stance, or from other causes that we deem so important and over which we spend so much time. Most of the shots missed

by duffer and star alike are missed through breaking
one of the few simple rules of the game: through moving the head or looking up, through pressing, or through
swaying the body at the wrong part of the swing.

In other words, most of these faults so commonly
found are mental faults—not physical ones. They
come from nervousness, overeagerness, lack of confidence, or some other condition of the mind. But
these faults seem to be missing in Vardon's make-up.
He isn't nervous, he isn't overeager, but he has perfect control of his mental faculties. If he didn't not
even his wonderful skill would make him a champion.
George Duncan is as brilliant as Vardon is. He can
play just as many varieties of shots. He can play
single rounds that no living man can beat. In one
match, some time back, Vardon was going at a
wonderful clip with a seventy-one and a seventy-two.
Duncan, playing like a whirlwind, had a seventy and
a sixty-nine. But Duncan hasn't the same control
of his nerves. Therefore Duncan has yet to win
a championship where Vardon has won six. So,

beyond all Vardon's great skill, wonderful style, and the rest of his physical perfections, the fact remains that he has reached the height by obtaining almost perfect control of his mental equipment, enabling him to play each shot as it ought to be played in the heat of the fight. If he had retained this same control of himself on the putting ground, and kept his putting up to the standard of his other play, he could have paralyzed all competition for the last fifteen years. As it is he has done well enough, and most of his success might be traced to a few simple rules:

1. Control of temper.
2. Refusing to worry over any bad lie or any hard luck.
3. Playing easily within himself and never pressing.
4. Playing always for the hole, even when two hundred yards away.
5. Studying his game and practising at every opportunity.
6. Making a point, even in practice, to follow all simple rules, such as keeping one's head still, looking at the ball, etc.

7.   Keeping the body under control until perfect timing is developed.

8.   Using an easy, natural, upright swing that stays as long as possible in line with the intended flight of the ball.

AYE, MON

A man may drive like an Eddie Ray,
Far and straight down the open way;
A man may come to a mashie shot
And push it up to the proper spot;
By hill and dune with the festive spoon
He may ramble on to the same old tune—
He may shoot one up to the far green's brink—
But what's the use when the putts won't sink ?

A man may be on his driving game
And smash them out to his soul's acclaim;
With whirring cleek and the niblick's swipe
His stuff be there and his form be ripe;
He may have the eye for a jigger try
And hold the line as a bird might fly;
From tee to green he may reap the crop—
But what's the use when his putts won't drop?

VIII

"BOY—BRING ME A NIBLICK!"

HARRY VARDON and other experts say that American golf courses have been under-trapped and too sparsely bunkered—and that to improve our golf we must add extra hazards and put a further tax upon a poorly played shot.

But what has the Tired Business Man to say about it? What is the inexpert opinion of the countless duffers who slice, hook, top, schlaff, foozle, and stutter their way around the course?

Even now in their dreams at night they see a mountain range to carry, an ocean to pitch over, and a fairway two feet wide flanked with bottomless grottoes inscribed with the Dantean legend: *"All Hope Abandon—Ye Who Enter Here."*

They know as their driver starts toward the ball

what the next spoken line will be, once the male-
dictions and the profanity are concluded.

"Boy—bring me a niblick."

A wasted command. The caddie had taken the
niblick out immediately after handing over the driver.
Habit brings on instinctive action. No great fore-
thought is required. The caddie's action was purely
subconscious, the result of constant repetition.

And yet in place of emerging from the wilderness
with the promised bunkerless land in sight, these,
whom we might call the duffers of the game, are
only on the threshold of their troubles. If what
Harry Vardon, Donald Ross, and others have to say
is correct, life for these hereafter will be just one
bunker after another—an endless chain effect of
earth thrown up and traps cut deeply.

There is no pleasure for us in saying what we feel
must be said to those who already spend three fourths
of their golfing time hidden from sight below the
earth's level, or blurred from view by some towering
bunker, where only the whirr of the niblick is heard

—that and language that no man shall ever see in print.

But "murder will out," as the saying is said to be. The news must be broken some time, so why not now—and here?

THE OBJECT OF GOLF

"The object of golf from now on," says Donald Ross, who has laid out seventy-three American courses, "will be toward an even greater science of stroke. Deep traps will be placed down the center, so that the golfer must shoot either to the right or left. To play well a man must have a wide variety of shots. More and more he will be forced to use his head as well as his hands and arms. More and more the golfer will have to have control over the club to insure direction or meet certain trouble."

The edict has gone forth that golf has become too easy, and that decided changes must be made.

Yet there are many golfers now like that visitor who plumped his tee shot into the trap guarding the

"BOY—BRING ME A NIBLICK!"

eighteenth green at Garden City. With his trusty niblick in his hand he disappeared from view. There soon followed the muffled sound of much thudding of sand—the echo of a strong-lunged man using even stronger language—and then the boding hush of silence. Three minutes—four minutes—five minutes his opponent waited above. Finally he could stand the strain no longer. "Why don't you drop your club and throw the ball out?" he yelled down in disgust.

"H——l," came the reply, with even more disgusted intonation—"that's what I've been trying to do for five minutes. What do you think I am—a Walsh or a Mathewson?"

This brings us again to the Tired Business Man, held responsible for so many foolish plays. We interviewed a large number of those whose scores range from 100 to 174 for eighteen holes, and the general verdict about trapping golf courses seemed to be about this:

"We go out for recreation and amusement—not

for a battle against all nature, riveted, bored, mounded, and hurled against us. We leave the office slightly tired and depressed, but jubilant in the thought of an afternoon outdoors. We reach the first tee buoyed up beyond measure, overrunning with joy. We come to the eighteenth tee a mass of shattered, wracked nerves, worn out in body and soul, with frayed tempers and our morals stunned.

"We come out to sport upon the Rhine—and they send us over the Rubicon. We come out to joy ride through Romany—and they drive us deep into Rome. We come out to play golf—and they make us hewers of earth and splashers of water. We come out to play with seven clubs—and after one shot from the tee they force us to fall back upon one."

THE PROBLEM OF THE GAME

It's quite a problem. The logic of the above sounds irresistible. Yet the advanced theorists, plugging steadily ahead with deeper pits and loftier hazards, merely point to the continued boom of the game and to the fact that the harder each course is made the more men curse, but the more anxious they are to play it again.

They can prove to you by statistics—by cold, clean facts—that the harder courses are the ones most eagerly sought by the greater number.

And undoubtedly they are correct in their viewpoint. The duffer, playing a 92 upon an easy course, raves with the savage fury of a wild man when he returns 110 at Garden City or Baltusrol, or 120 at the National.

He imagines that he will never play a course like this again, that he will quit the game first. But the next day, playing his own easy course, he suddenly misses the thrill which came from playing one shot correctly beyond such an avalanche of trouble, and at the first chance he returns again to tackle the problem, in an attempt to make a better showing.

The average golfer, even the average high-handicap player, not only likes but takes pride in a well-trapped championship course. If he belongs to an easy course he tells the name of his golf club in a most humble tone. But if he is a member of some club claiming a championship course—such as Baltusrol, Garden City, Myopia, or Brookline—though his best mark over that course be 117, still will his pride in belonging to that club be unusually keen.

There are exceptions, of course. At the East Lake course in Atlanta, Georgia, a bunker was erected in front of a certain tee, calling for a carry of some 170 yards.

One of the club members, a short driver, had been playing golf for five years, when he came to this shot and promptly plunked the ball into the bunker's side. On four successive rounds he found this same trouble. The day after, in place of playing around as usual, he took two dozen balls, a caddie, and a driver, and went to this tee, working for two hours in a vain attempt to hit the ball over. For nearly a month he kept this up. And then one day, after an extended spray of sunshine had baked out the course, a half-topped shot with a supporting wind behind carried the ball on a bound over the bunker's side.

"My life's ambition at golf," he said, "is satisfied. Now I am through," and he has never swung a club since.

TRAPPING NEEDED

In football no offence of the right sort can be developed unless it be trained against a strong defence. In baseball no club can be developed at bat unless it face high-class pitching. And in golf no first-class player can be developed unless he is given a chance to play over a course calling for control and a variety of shots. The golfer who plays over an untrapped course, where bad shots are rarely ever penalized, has a tendency to become careless—and to lose control. For control can only be developed where there is a penalty waiting for a misplay.

Too many American courses are not properly bunkered for a tee shot. They fail to develop control with the wood as a first-class course should do. And it is on this account that American golfers, invading England, find so much trouble. They are unaccustomed to the high winds and the more extensive trapping, and lack the steady control to meet the occasion.

And yet there is a limit: the Tired Business Man. The average golfer is willing to take a chance—to accept a penalty for a poorly played shot, he will tell you. It may be best for the game—for an improved game—to adorn the course with yearly added difficulties—but is it best for the nation's nerves, morals, and happiness?

No wonder the Tired Business Man is so called. That is why he is tired.

A nation's wealth, as judged by Adam Smith, is measured by its happiness.

Can a nation be happy with so large a percentage of its population spending so large a percentage of its spare time in traps and bunkers?

The violet-stained feet of young Spring come dancing across the green hills. The plains throw off winter's winding sheet of snow to ripple and wander away in the sunlight.   There is new life in the land, and joy abounding everywhere.

But above the singing birds, the wind song of the trees, the joyous rippling melody of the brooks, there sounds and sweeps a vast cataclysm of anguish that is poignant, and language that is horrible to hear. It comes from the depths of the earth—from the crests of many mounds—from hazards of water and swamps of grass.   It comes with a snarl and a rasp of tone and a curse upon all living things.

It comes from the soul of those in mortal agony—in death-dealing rage—and it comes in the wake of that last line of spoken despair:

“Boy, bring me a niblick!”

THE GOLFER SPEAKS

If I should die to-night,
   And as with folded arms in death I lay
Some beaten rival whom I'd put to flight
   Should bend above my resting corpse and say:
"Old boy, you won by greater skill and pluck,
   You had me trimmed from putting green to tee,
You had the stuff but I had all the luck
   I should have been six down instead of three."

If he said that,
   Although my soul was even then a spook
I'd rise at once in my large, white cravat
   To get one look at him—one final look,
I'd make him say it over word for word
   Till I was sure that I had rightly heard;
Yes, I'd rise up within my shroud, and then—
   I'd drop back dead again.

                    (With apologies to Ben King)

[184]

BEATING 'EM TO IT

Yes, pal, I know just how it was—you should have
won a mile;

You had him trimmed ten ways on form and twenty
ways on style;

You had him stewed into a trance—you had him strung
until

You went and blew a ten-inch putt where something
tipped the pill;

A putt you wouldn't miss again the whole blank summer long—

A pop-eyed pipe to anchor—am I right or am I wrong?

I get you, pal—don't say a word—he wasn't in your
class;

You had no less than twelve bad kicks that plunked
you in the grass;

*While you were straight upon the pin, he foozled every
  shot,*

*But somehow skidded on the green and gathered in the
  pot;*

*No, not a word; I know, old top—your case is nothing
  new—*

*I know, because each time I lose they beat me that way,
  too.*

IX

THE HIGH COST OF GOLFING

MR. WILLIAM JONES belongs to that type of citizenry who receives a fair salary— enough to live on with something on the side. But to reach this point he has worked a little bit harder and a little bit longer than he should have worked without mixing in some recreation. He finds at last that he must get this recreation, and after looking over the field he decides to take up golf, upon the advice of certain friends who lift the limit in recommending this game.

So Jones goes in for the game, joins a club, secures a golfing outfit, and plays at least twice a week for about eight months out of the year. What has this year's golf cost him? Jones doesn't know. Neither does Smith. Neither does Brown. They only know it was worth it in the way of added pleasure and of savings in doctors' bills and in the way of added energy applied to work.

But for the benefit of Mr. Jones, average citizen and average golfer, we can tell him just about what it cost individually, and perhaps jar him a bit with the total annual golfing cost as applied to the United States alone.

THE FIRST YEAR

What does it cost to play golf? In the way of extremes, anything you want. You can enter, only you probably can't, the most exclusive club in the country for an initiation fee of $5,000. Or you can take up the game on a public course where the fee is nothing, or perhaps one dollar, and where no dues are required.

Around the New York and Chicago districts, where over 180 clubs are represented, the average dues are $90 a year, with the average initiation fee at $100. But a fair average over the entire golfing realm would be considerably less, say about one half.

We will say, then, that Jones takes up golf, enters a club, pays a $50 initiation fee, $50 annual dues, buys the needed seven clubs, and plays twice a week, Saturdays and Sundays, for eight months of the year. Being an average citizen, he will need the seven clubs for the average player—driver, brassie, cleek, mid-iron, mashie, niblick, and putter. These seven clubs at $2.50 each will cost him $17.50. A great many golfers carry less, but a great many also carry more, adding a spoon and a jigger to the above list. So seven is a fair average.

If he plays twice a week for eight months he will travel the course about 64 times, which will require on an average about three dozen golf balls, or one to every 36 holes. (Please remember that in all this we are taking up the average case.) So Jones must pay at least $20 for the number of balls he uses. His carfare will be at least $20; around the larger cities it will be much more, and around the smaller cities less, but this is the Average City. And to this must be added a caddie charge of 40 cents a round, or about $25 for the season.

So at the end of the first year Mr. William Jones, average citizen and average golfer, playing in the average town, can figure up his expenses as follows:

Initiation fee	$ 50.00
Annual dues	50.00
Balls	20.00
Clubs	17.50
Carfare	20.00
Caddie pay	25.00
Total	$182.50

This doesn't include money paid to the golf professional for instruction at one dollar an hour; golf toggery in the way of shoes, cap, and other details, nor does it include any part or parcel of expenditures around the Nineteenth Hole. It is merely a list of the necessary charges. After the first year the initiation fee is removed and the cost of clubs is reduced, bringing the actual cost down to an average of $120 a year, or about two dollars for each round played through a season of eight months. There will be thousands who will spend three or four times this amount; and there will be other thousands who will spend less. But for a general average these figures will not be very far away.

HIGH INTO THE MILLIONS

The average cost of $120 doesn't seem very large. It isn't, when considered alone. But when this cost is multiplied by all those playing golf in the United States, it is then that one suddenly wakes to the enormous amount of money spent upon the game— far more than is spent upon any other sport in the nation.

This may sound like a joke to a good many. More money spent on golf than upon baseball, with all these high-priced players and all these big stadiums? Yes, a good bit more. And we believe we can show it to the satisfaction of all.

As far as the listed number of organizations is concerned, there are 1,300 golf clubs now in the United States. There are many others not listed in this report, and there are certainly a great many more being constructed, for each season finds a large number of additions. These 1,300 clubs have a playing, or rather an active playing, list of 350,000 members. There is no way of telling just how many dabble at golf occasionally, but there are certainly several hundred thousand more. Some expert statisticians have figured that at least a million people are now playing golf in the United States; but this seems to be a trifle high. As an estimate, 350,000 active players isn't far wrong, for each club will average 250. Many clubs run up to 800 and 1,000 members, and few fall below 200, so 250 to the club is certainly a low estimate.

ALMOST A WAR FUND

Figured then on the basis of 350,000 active golfers, at the average cost summed up of $120 a year, the total amount spent on golf each season runs up to $42,000,000, and this exclusive of the $17,500,000 paid in for initiation fees!

This seems to be an incredible amount of money to be paid out for one sport, one among many others, but if anything we have underestimated the average cost, as the average golfer will understand and bear us out. And if to this is added the amount paid for shoes, golf toggery, and the purchased buoyancy of the Nineteenth Hole, the sum total easily exceeds $50,000,000 each year.

Of this amount the largest individual item is in dues, which amount to something like $17,500,000 annually.

WHERE IT GOES

Where does all this money go? That part, too, is easily enough answered. With 1,300 clubs listed, each club will average 100 acres. Very few are under this and a great many have much more space. This means at least 130,000 acres devoted to the art of losing golf balls.

[193]

These 130,000 acres are with few exceptions close to some town or large city and are all the center of popular residence neighbourhoods. The moment a section of land is staked off for a golf course, adjoining lots all take on greatly increased value. For the 100 acres necessary for the golf club, of course, widely different prices are charged, but it is safe to say that the average acre on a golf course is worth $600. This means a matter of $78,000,000 worth of real estate tied up in golf, and another $20,000,000 tied up in clubhouses.

The purchase of golf territory and the enormous amounts of money required to fix up and keep a course in repair take most of the annual fund spent upon the game. For example, two good courses in the east are Nassau and Englewood. The land on one cost $175,000 and on the other $165,000. Add to this the $50,000 or $60,000 necessary to lay out and build up a course, and then follows the $10,000 a year needed to keep the fairway and putting greens in good condition for play, and it is easy enough to see where the money goes. Many millions are spent each year in the upkeep of the 1,300 courses.

A SEVENTY-TWO-THOUSAND-DOLLAR GREEN

There may be more expensive putting greens somewhere around the golfing landscape, but certainly one of the most expensive is that of the third hole at the Crescent Athletic Club course. This hole overlooks the bay and is situated high upon the Shore Drive, Long Island. It is less than 100 feet square, and yet $72,000 has been offered for it. So golfers who top their approaches to this green miss a very rich landing-place.

Another pair of expensive holes laid out are at the Brookline Country Club, Boston, Massachusetts, where Ouimet won the American Open Championship two years ago. These are the ninth and tenth holes, and for good parts of the way they were cut from solid rock, to permit an opening from tee to green. It is figured that with all the work required, necessitating an unusual amount of blasting, the two holes cost at least $50,000. So those who imagine that golf holes are made by merely sinking a tin cup in some fairly smooth place have another guess coming.

FOR THE PROFESSIONALS

The successful laying out of a golf course requires the work of an expert, one who understands how to develop the widest range of shots, and when his map is finished the work of getting this course into shape takes a big force of men and at least two or three years before the grass is of the desired carpetlike quality. And one can figure upon at least $7,800,000 a year needed to keep these courses in shape.

Another large item of golfing expenditure is brought in by the different professionals in charge. Each club has at least one professional, who has various duties, the two main assignments being to conduct a shop where clubs and balls are sold and to furnish instruction to such members as may desire to advance further or to get back upon their game.

Each professional will average at least $100 a

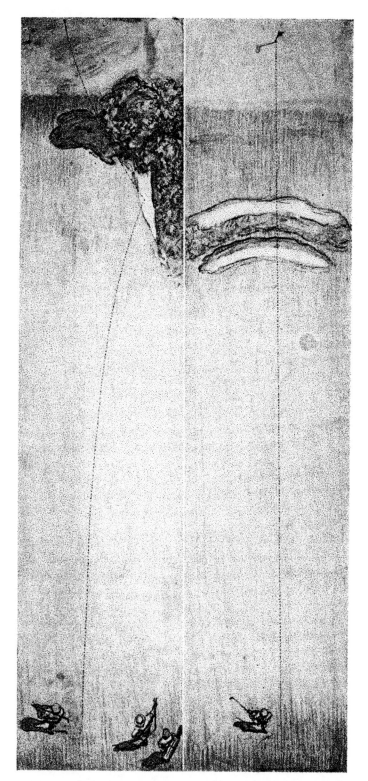

LICE THAT WON A CHAMPIONSHIP   A 400-YARD HOLE IN TWO!

y some strange freak Hilton's ball   The diagram shows a 160-yard "hole

month, or $1,200 a year, which means a salary out-
lay of $1,300,000. It seems almost impossible to
mention any golf expense account without going into
the millions. In addition to this fixed salary, the
professional gets what profit he can obtain from the
sale of balls and golf clubs, and is also paid at a rate
of one dollar an hour for instruction. Many professionals enjoy fine incomes from these combined
sources, and for instruction alone it is probable that
$750,000 is paid out annually by those who desire a
slice removed and a pull inserted, or who would like
to play an occasional mashie shot within thirty or
forty yards of the pin.

There is no better way to get back upon one's
game or to develop a game than by this method, and
this fact is becoming recognized to such an extent
that most of our pros. are kept very busy teaching
from morning to night, and many of them are able to
make as high as $4,000 or $5,000 a year.

This pressure of instruction is undoubtedly cutting
into the tournament success of many of our best

players. Many of them have little or no time at all for practice. They are kept busy giving lessons from 8 A. M. until 6 P. M., and get in only an occasional round. Most of these get nothing like the play and practice obtained by a great many of our leading amateurs, which accounts to a certain extent for the small tournament margin between the pro. and the amateur of late.

On the other hand, Vardon, the British champion, rarely ever gives instruction, plays in tournaments constantly, and so is, of course, far better able to give a good account of himself in any championship engagement.

CONCERNING FEES AND DUES

Earlier in this article we set the average for initiation fees at $50. This estimate is probably too low. Very few clubs have an entrance fee below $50, whereas any number range not only far beyond $50, but to financial altitudes almost unbelievable.

Out in St. Louis there is a golf club known as the

Log Cabin, where the membership list is limited to twenty-five. And to get in, the new member must produce $5,000, in return for which he is of course given bonds of the club. But the $5,000 is regarded as an entrance or initiation fee.

Chicago has a new club, the Old Elm, where the fee for entering as a member is $1,500. There are other clubs in St. Louis, Chicago, New York, and Philadelphia where a fee of $400 is required. But around New York most clubs charge $100 for a fee, and place their dues at from $75 to $90 a year. In smaller cities the average fee is $40 or $50, with dues about the same.

There is probably no club in the country that gives as much for its money as the Atlanta Athletic Club, which harbours the best golf course in the South, and where golf is the main feature. This club charges only $50 a year for dues. And for this money the members get a championship golf course, a long line of tennis courts, a lake for boating, a rifle range, and in addition a downtown house where a big gymnasium is provided, and where all indoor games are well looked after and excellent reading-rooms are established.

The membership here is 1,000, with a long waiting list attached.

COST OF CLUBS

Another important item is the money spent in golf clubs. These clubs cost from $2.50 to $3.50 each. Their shafts are of seasoned hickory and cost the professionals at wholesale rates 40 cents each. This, with the wooden or iron heads and the leather grip required, runs the actual cost of making them well up above a dollar.

These shafts are hard to get, for many of them are too whippy, and are not able to stand the terrific strain under which they are used. Only the best wood can last for any length of time. On an average, each golfer will use seven clubs. There are many who will use only five; but there are more who continue adding clubs to their stock, until any number have from ten to twenty clubs in their locker before they are able to get just the clubs they want.

With an average of seven clubs for 350,000 golfers, at $2.50 to the club, we have an outlay of $6,125,000 spent for clubs. Each year a club or two is added, and if only one club was purchased each season after the original investment, we would have an annual expenditure of $875,000 in this department of the game alone.

It is no easy matter for one to secure just the set of clubs one wants. After a few weeks' or a few months' play with any set, a golfer takes strong likes and equally strong dislikes to clubs. If he has a club that he believes doesn't suit him and in which he has no confidence, although it isn't the club's fault, he might as well start to looking around for another to take its place. He will never be satisfied until he does. There are many golfers who carry from ten to fifteen clubs. There is one star who carries at least twenty, and few caddies make any extended effort to get his bag.

It is just as well for one to have a driver, brassie, spoon, cleek or driving iron, mid-iron, jigger, mashie, niblick, and putter, a total of nine clubs.

Many carry a mashie-niblick and a heavy niblick as well, which would bring the list to ten, and which would incur starting expenditures of $22.50 for clubs alone.

Leading professionals in tournament play always go armed for any emergency that might arrive. In a big match played in England, James Braid, five times Open Champion, put his second shot into a deep trap right up against the wall. The green, a fast, sloping one, began at the edge of the trap. It was necessary that Braid get out, and yet equally important that he should not get too far. So in place of using his regular niblick he reached in his bag for a club that looked more like a shovel than anything else. This club had a big, round, heavy, iron head, and with it Braid struck a mighty blow at least four inches back of the ball, with the result that it popped out of the sand, just cleared the wall, and lay within two feet of the hole. So at times freak clubs are required for freak shots.

Chick Evans, the crack Chicago golfer, at one time carried four putters around with him, which was a bad idea, as it destroyed confidence in any one putter, and left him uncertain at each putt.

But the idea must not be got from this that everything in golf and about golf is overexpensive. Public courses offer those who love the game and lack the price a chance to play for almost nothing. There are golfers on public courses who have kept track of all expenditures, and have found that they were able to play a full season on less than twenty dollars, and this included carfare. These are the golfers who show the grip of the game upon all who take it.

FOR LOVE OF THE GAME

Here is an example of what many of these go up against to get in their favourite diversion:

A certain golfer in New York one day decided to play on Sunday at the public course at Van Cortlandt

Park. He had never tried it before, although he understood that a good many had the same Sunday scheme. On this particular Sunday he decided to get out early, and so get well ahead of the field, in order to get around quickly and so get in two full rounds before noon. To make things doubly sure he decided to get out by five o'clock in the morning. He arrived at 5 A. M., but he didn't lead the field that day.

To his great surprise he found something over ninety golfers ahead of him, all ready to start, and some of these had been on hand for well over an hour, or before four o'clock. A man must love a game who, after a hard week's work, is willing to get up at 3 A. M. on his rest day and wait several hours to get started at his game, waiting for daylight and for the line to melt until his turn came to step up and place the small white ball upon its resting-place of sand.

ON PUBLIC COURSES

There are 110 golf courses within the New York, or what is known as the Metropolitan, District.

These can take care of 50,000 golfers with ease. One would think all these courses would take up all the golfing talent to be found in one city. But at Van Cortlandt Park this last summer a fee of one dollar was charged for the privilege of playing on the course, and 6,600 golfers applied for the necessary permission. If a golfer attempted to start at this course by arriving at eight o'clock Sunday morning, it would be well on into the afternoon before his turn would come.

There is as much, or more, interest at the Jackson Park course in Chicago, where it has been figured up that over 500,000 rounds were played last year. This widespread interest in golf has started an upbuilding of public courses in many other cities. For golf, in private clubs, is still too expensive in America. Over in England and Scotland some of the greatest courses are public courses, and it is possible there for workmen making low wages to enjoy a round of golf at least twice a week over a very fine course.

America as yet has nothing like this. Its public courses are still far too few, and not up to the standard that develops the best golf. But this condition is improving as public officials are beginning to realize the growing love for the game among the public at large.

PAY OF CADDIES

The money made by caddies out of golf is one of the most interesting features of the game. These boys range from youngsters only ten years old to others who are from eighteen to twenty. Through the week only about ten or fifteen of these are kept busy to each course, but on Saturdays and Sundays— especially on Saturdays and holidays, as many clubs have refused to let caddies work on Sunday—there must be fully 100,000 boys earning from fifty cents to a dollar for their one or two rounds. During the playing season, especially the spring and fall seasons, golfers throughout the United States must pay out at least $60,000 a week in caddie fees, which is no small item for young boys, who, however, earn every cent they make, despite many complaints they receive.

No, the caddie isn't overpaid. He is out in the open, leading a healthy life; but the golfer is inclined at times to be selfish and thoughtless, and boys are blamed for the loss of golf balls that an Argus couldn't follow or find, not if he had two hundred eyes. Golfers should be much more careful than they are in their general behaviour, meaning both deed and word, in the presence of their caddies who, being much younger, are so much more easily influenced.

It is hard to say just how much is paid out for caddie fees in the course of an entire season, but it wouldn't be far wrong to say this annual bill is at least $3,000,000. And $3,000,000 is not an inconsiderable amount for even the youth of America to earn in the course of a year.

These statistics have been made up after a careful study of the situation and after obtaining all records available. They show what a tremendous industry the ancient Scottish game has grown to be in a country where twenty years ago it was almost unknown, with very few devotees.

Ten years ago in the United States golf was only getting a good start. And yet here to-day we have $100,000,000 invested in the game through real estate, clubhouses, and general improvements; we are spending as a nation $50,000,000 a year upon its pursuit; we are furnishing pleasure to over 350,000 players, and employment, including men and boys, to over 300,000 people.

In addition to that we have given up 130,000 acres of our most valuable soil to this game, which has grown with such amazing rapidity that it has been hard to keep pace in the way of course building, as any number of clubs have already passed their limits and have waiting lists of formidable sizes on hand. And yet, in the face of all this, there are those who are inclined to doubt the wonderful grip this game has upon the nation, a nation that within the next ten years will double its golfing contingent and will spend close to $100,000,000 a year in keeping up the game. It takes something of a game, something beyond a mere fad, to reach such proportions. In fact, it takes golf.

THE GOLF WIDOW SPEAKS

You have kicked in with a serum for the Great White
  Plague;
You have uppercut the Typhus on the jaw;
You have copped an anæsthetic
To relieve the diphtheretic,
And the rest of it you've cut out with a saw.
But tell me, gentle doctors, ere the mortal coil is off,
Is there nothing you've discovered in the medicated
  trough
That may curb the raging fever of this game called
  " goff?"

You have cantered into Gangrene with a knock-out
  punch;
You have hammered Scarlet Fever to the ropes;
You have even found the answer
To a mild degree of Cancer,

And you've killed the drug enticement of the dopes.
But tell me, learned doctors, is there nothing you can do
For hydrophobic horrors in the heads of husbands who
Can only rave of Stymies and a Perfect FollowThrough?

X

WHEN LOVELY WOMAN STOOPS TO GOLF

THE female of the species may or may not be deadlier than the male. We have no intention of debating this unhappy question with Mr. Kipling. But, in the matter of tournament golf play, the female temperament is not only far less deadly than the male, but far less unbending, rigid— and boring. It may not be quite so effective in regard to general results, but in the way of elasticity, buoyancy, and fun, there can be no comparison.

Some time ago Miss Muriel Dodd and Miss Gladys Ravenscroft, two very eminent English golfers, had just finished a one-day tournament at Englewood, N. J., in which, possibly, seventy-five women had taken part. I had followed, that afternoon, the leading entries, who included, in addition to Miss Dodd and Miss Ravenscroft, Miss Marion Hollins of New York.

On the way back to the clubhouse I was vaguely conscious of a wide difference between the general atmosphere of that tournament and of tournaments conducted by the sterner sex. There was, I knew, quite a difference, but I was not sure what the difference was until two ladies, just in front of me, solved the problem for me.

"Now this," said one of them, "is what I call *real* sport. Tournaments handled by men have always left me with an awful headache. They made me feel as if I didn't dare to breathe. They were so idiotically solemn about it themselves that I felt I was at a funeral. But to-day everything was so different. When Miss Dodd missed a shot, she laughed, and the same with Miss Ravenscroft and Miss Hollins. And we all laughed with them. The players had a good time and so did the spectators. It was sport—not war."

The facts had been most correctly stated. Among

the women who played at Englewood that day, especially among the best of them, there had been a total absence of that morose masculine stolidity which characterizes all of our male-conducted tournaments. Both from experience and from close observation I can say that men get very little real enjoyment out of tournament golf. They may quarrel with this statement, but the truth of it is undeniable.

When men play in a qualifying round, the spectacle is not only impressive, but dreary. A topped mashie shot into a bunker brings to the player an anguish beyond all words. A sliced drive means intense suffering, while a sliced putt, close to the hole, pierces the poor man's heart with the poisoned arrow of a woe that may not be assuaged. When men play in tournaments they move from tee to tee and from green to green with the gravity that one might feel in marching out to bury the body of a friend.

The sky may be blue, the earth may be green, and

the surrounding hills may be white or crimson, but their strained vision looks only ahead—to the ball and to the flag in the distance beyond. Of friendly conversation there is little or none. They are at heart much like the two Scotchmen, one of whom at the sixteenth hole finally said "Dom," as he missed a putt, only to be berated by his partner for being a chatterbox.

Now, I don't mean to say that women esteem it an abiding bliss to top a mashie into a bunker, or to miss a short putt, but if one of these unhappy events *should* take place, it is not nearly so tragic a circumstance as when it takes place with a man. And if any annoyance is shown or felt by women, it is quickly dispelled by a laugh or by some good-natured comment.

That day at Englewood, when Miss Ravenscroft or Miss Dodd or Miss Hollins had driven from the tee, they were off down the course, laughing and chatting together as if they were solely bent on being happy, and not on winning a silver mug.

"Well," you might reply in rebuttal, "their game shows the effect of introducing such a dangerous element as fun into tournament play."

Quite so, and yet that afternoon, with a strong wind scurrying across the course and conditions against good medal play, Miss Ravenscroft returned an 81 on her first round trip. Her mind had been sufficiently upon the game to reach the sixth hole, 530 yards long, in two shots with a very favouring wind; a result that should satisfy the mental concentration of any masculine player in the land.

That tournament was not the only exhibition of the feminine golfing temperament which I have in mind.

Shortly before the Englewood match, the Woman's Golf Championship of the United States had been staged at Wilmington, Delaware.

Miss Dodd and Miss Ravenscroft were entered, and it was almost certain that one of the two visitors would win. They finally came together for a great test match. Under the same conditions, two men, on the night before, would have been keyed up to a high nervous pitch, sleepless perhaps, and certainly under a heavy mental strain. Here was a championship at stake for which two young ladies had travelled 3,000 miles. Let us see how impressive the occasion was to them. Well, on the night before the tournament, they went to a dance, stayed there until three o'clock, and took the first tee on the next morning as if they were only off for a good tramp together. Miss Dodd played very badly and was soundly beaten, but, in so far as any dispiriting effect upon her could be discerned, she was having the time of her young life. When she topped a drive she almost invariably laughed, complimented her rival on a good shot, and then the two together went arm in arm down the course with the loser in as good a humour as the winner.

When the match was over the loser was effusive in her congratulations, and if she was insincere her form was as remarkable as an actress as it was as a golfer, and—according to no less an authority than

Harry Vardon—her golfing form is not surpassed by the best man player alive. She had only recently won the Woman's Championship of Great Britain, so it was not a case of her submitting to an expected defeat.

It is not my purpose here entirely to indorse the feminine attitude as exemplified in the instances mentioned above, but if the average masculine golfer could come a trifle closer to that attitude he would not only have a much better time, but, in my humble opinion, play a better game. The strain on him would not be so heavy. There would be a greater absence of that rigidity of swing which comes from overtaut nerves.

To take his play just a bit less seriously would bring a needed relaxation of muscle, and it is the absence of any such relaxation which accounts, in the main, for the high scoring in so many medal-play rounds. Golfers, easily capable of doing an 81 or an 82 in friendly rounds, return cards of 90 or 91 in tournaments, curse their luck, and wonder why it is that they fell down so badly. The answer is, obviously, that they were getting their 81's and 82's when they were playing golf in easy-going rounds, in rounds, that is, when they were playing in much the same spirit as that shown by Miss Dodd and Miss Ravenscroft at Wilmington and Englewood.

But regardless of the matter of scores, think of the fun the men are missing! After all, isn't it better to be able to laugh, or at least to smile, over a missed bit of luck, than to mutter morose and meaningless profanities because an approach that stopped twenty feet beyond the pin didn't have the ordinary decency to hit it and stop dead to the hole?

THE DUFFER'S DREAM

WITH ANY NECESSARY APOLOGIES

One night a Duffer dreamed that he had died
And that his wretched, bally soul had skied
To Heaven's gate, where, finding it was locked,
He clamoured "Fore" and hammered, rapped, and
  knocked.

"Who comes," St. Peter cried, "with all that din?"
"A Duffer," cried the soul, "please let me in."
"And what is that," he heard the good saint say,
"That you should hear the golden harps at play,
What have you done upon that earth so drear
That you should mingle with the angels here?
Put me adjacent to a Duffer's fate"—
And this reply came drifting through the Gate—

THE DUFFER'S DREAM

"A Duffer's fate?   I pray you bend an ear
And be prepared, O Saint, to shed a tear;
For thirteen years the ancient green I baffed,
Sliced, hooked, and foozled, topped and smeared and
*   schlaffed,*
Spending my days in bunkers, traps, and worse
Dividing time between a sob and curse;
Losing each time I struck a swinging blow
A new white ball at sixty cents a throw,
Until a wreck, with tangled nerves awry,
I had naught left except an alibi.

"A Duffer's fate?   To work your soul apart
And then get worse each time you make a start;
To be ashamed at any time or place
To look your anguished caddie in the face;
To know your friends, each time that you alight,
Are diving swiftly from your anxious sight;
To get an 'eight,' a 'seven,' and a 'ten,'
A 'nine,' a 'six,' and then an 'eight' again;

To flub your drive and take three putts or more,
While those behind are loudly yelling 'Fore'—
To know each year the selfsame bitter lot—
You have the facts—do I get in, or not?"

"Here is the key," St. Peter said. "Come through—
Heaven, I think, was built for such as you;
Choose any harp among these scenes of mirth—
O blighted soul, you had your Hell on earth."

RARE SPECIES

I've met a beggar in the street who scorned my proffered
  gift;

I've come upon a worn-out tramp who would not take a
  lift;

I've met a fighter who exclaimed amid the roaring din:

"I fell before a better bloke without a chance to win";

I've met a guy who never heard of Teddy or of Ty—

Who never heard of Johnson's speed or Baker's batting
  eye;

But though I've been around the world and lamped
  within my scope

A million weird varieties beyond the purling dope,

Including scribes who spurned all cash and merely
  wrote for fame,

In all my life I've never met a golfer "on his game."

XI

GOLF NERVE UNDER FIRE

OUR duffer friend, William Smith, decides to enter an invitation golf tournament, of which many dozens are held all over the country from April to January.

Smith knows that his best game is not likely to beat an 87 or 88, and that his average game is about 93 to 95. But he figures to himself that with a 92 or 93 he can easily get into the third or fourth "sixteen," and perhaps have a chance to win in one of those lower divisions.

When his starting time arrives he walks up to the first tee, takes a practice swing, and then, as he addresses the ball, suddenly finds that his nervous system is paralyzed. There is probably a gallery looking on (galleries generally gather around the first tee to see the start), and poor Smith feels immediately that every eye is watching every move of his swing. He is so anxious to get away a good shot that he lifts his head, tops or smears the drive, and then looks around longingly for some hole to dive into and hide. The disgrace is keen—in his own imagination. He has lost his nerve, has shown that he was a quitter by blowing up on the first shot.

Or perhaps he gets away a good drive, marches on jauntily after the ball with head up and cheerful heart, reaches the green on his next shot, and then, after laying an approach putt up within two feet, misses. The chances are that he will continue missing these putts right along thereafter, if this is his first tournament, for all confidence will then have been destroyed.

For Mr. Smith, duffer, we have a few words of comfort to impart. We may give him a chance to cheer up a bit, and to lose some of his depression over an apparent lack of nerve under fire. To explain our point we will shift the scene.

THE WINNING SHOT

WHEN THE STRAIN HIT A CHAMPION

We will shift the scene to Sunningdale, England, near the city of London. The tournament under way is for the St. George's Vase, one of the biggest tournaments of the year. Out from London and suburbs a crowd of at least seven thousand golf followers have come to follow two great stars. One of these stars is Harold Hilton, then British Amateur Champion. The other is Francis Ouimet, then American Open Champion.

Ouimet had already proved himself to be one of the golfing phenomena of the game. He had gone out against Vardon and Ray at Brookline before, and with the finest nerve I have ever seen had beaten them for the American title. Here, at last, every one said, is the golfer of iron nerve, the golfer who doesn't know what nervousness means. For had he not played Vardon and Ray off their feet without showing a quiver, without a break in his play from first to last?

But the scene is now at Sunningdale. With seven thousand looking on, Ouimet stepped up to the tee. The crowd was preparing to look far down the course to see one of those 250-yard shots leave a white streak against the sky. Ouimet swung at the ball, lifted his head, struck with the heel of his club, and spun off a shot, half-topped, through a portion of the crowd. It was almost a clean miss. Why? Well, Ouimet said, shortly after the match, that he was so nervous that he could hardly hold a club in his hand. And yet Ouimet, I know, has as fine a golfing nerve and as fine a temperament for play as any golfer in the game.

ANOTHER NERVE SHOCK

For the benefit of Mr. Smith, duffer, who deplores his lack of nerve control, I might shift the scene again. The leading actor on this occasion is myself. It was the night before the British Amateur Championship at Sandwich. I had gone over two months before to make ample preparation for this big international event. I had been playing the best golf of my life. I had at least nine years' tournament experience behind me, and I had played in a British championship before. After dinner I retired fairly early to get a good night's sleep for the big test next day, when I was to play my first match. Eleven o'clock came, but no sleep. Twelve o'clock, and I I was still awake. At one o'clock my eyes were wide open and every nerve in my body jumping sideways. At seven o'clock the next morning I got up without having closed my eyes. This is offered in no sense as any alibi. It is merely a statement of fact. The long siege of preparation, the knowledge of the importance of the occasion, combined with outside worries, had torn into my nervous system with a crash that might have been made by the shell of a sixteen-inch gun.

I was a beaten man before I walked to the tee, and beaten that early for the first time in my life. On the Sunday before I had played Sandwich in seventy-four strokes, my last preliminary round. That day, Palmer, the Irish champion, returned an 88, fourteen strokes worse than I had played twenty-four hours before—and yet this was enough to beat by the margin of two. For I had a 90, by all odds the worse round of golf I had played since leaving American soil two months before. And yet, before that I had always been able to play my best golf under fire.

ENCOURAGEMENT FOR THE DUFFER

These two examples are offered as a starter by way of encouragement to Mr. Smith, duffer at large. For I can tell him truthfully that no golfer ever lived who was not harassed at one time or another by a nervous upset that wrecked his game. It is simple enough to call a man a quitter. But that expression would never be used if it had to come from a man who had never lost his nerve or control of his nerves in his life.

There are no exceptions to this statement. And by all odds the most interesting study of golf is the study of golf nerves and golf temperament as applied to individual cases.

In the first place, just what is golf temperament? Is it power of concentration? Is it mainly a lack of nerves, or a control of nerves, or possession of nerve? I have seen some of the nerviest men I have ever known miss short putts in tight matches through sheer nervousness. But there must be some ingredient here that decides the battle where two golfers of equal skill meet, and one is always the winner through a greater steadiness against the test. The best temperament has been called the "wooden temperament," which means lack of nerves. This may be true, but who is possessor of this so-called "wooden temperament," save at rare intervals? In my own case I am supposed to have very few nerves at work, to have nothing but ice in my veins when at play. On the contrary, I am often highly nervous and have made some of my best shots when my nerves seemed to be jumping sideways. That day against Palmer I couldn't have made a three-foot putt if the hole had been twice as large. Yet in other tournaments I have gone in feeling nervous and have managed to keep myself well in check, which means that I **man-aged** to keep my eye on the ball **and to keep con-trol** of my timing.

HOW TRAVIS WORKS IT

The same is supposed to be **true of Walter** J. Travis. It is **the** general opinion that **he** hasn't a nerve in **his** body, that nothing upsets him. He has played in more tournaments than any other golfer in America, but for all that Travis is full of nerves. It is only by wonderful powers of concentration that he keeps these nerves in check. And he turns the **trick** in this fashion:

In playing a friendly match, with absolutely nothing at stake, Travis plays as grimly as if the championship of the world depended upon each shot. He schools himself to concentration day after day and year after year, and so, when he enters a tournament, **he** is trained in nerve control. But there are oc-casions recorded when his nerves, even under all this schooling, broke away from his grip and left him as helpless against the test as others known to be nervous.

A QUADRANGULAR NERVE TEST

One of the most striking quadrangular cases of nerve tests or temperament tests, might be shown in the rivalries of four great English golfers—Hilton, Harris, Ball, and the late Freddie Tait. Harris is a great golfer, yet he could never play his best against Hilton, who beat him repeatedly. Hilton is one of the greatest of all amateurs, yet he always found both Tait and Ball almost impossible to beat. Tait could beat Hilton but he could rarely beat Ball. When Hilton went against Harris he played with supreme confidence, expecting to win, and always won. When he played against Ball, although a much better player than Ball is or was, he generally came in beaten. Why? He could never explain it. He only felt that he could beat one and that he couldn't beat the other.

To my mind, if there was ever a man in golf possessed of so-called iron nerve, or lack of nerves, it was John Ball, eight times Amateur Champion of Great Britain. He was as stolid as a rock at all times. Apparently a tournament meant nothing to him. It has been recorded how, on one occasion, just before a final round for the British Championship was to be started, he was found working in his garden, with no thought of golf in his head, and he only came away to play his match with great reluctance.

Yet I saw even the iron-hearted Ball show the effect of a nervous upset. In the British Championship at Sandwich he had come to the eighteenth hole one up. All he needed here against his opponent was a halved hole to win the match. Playing this hole Ball was only twelve feet from the pin in two, while his rival was off the edge of the green. There seemed to be no chance for Ball to be beaten. He had a half at least sewed up. But in my entire golf career I don't believe I ever saw a man take as long for one shot as Ball's opponent did from the edge of the green. He must have taken at least five minutes, and it seemed like five hours before he was through.

He finally chipped up within three feet of the cup. By this time Ball had evidently become nervous over the long delay, for he putted only halfway, missed the next putt, lost the hole and then the match, on the nineteenth green.

EVERYBODY DOES IT

Yes, Mr. Smith, duffer, can take cheer in the thought that he isn't alone in this lack of nerve control. He is not only not alone, but he is with the vast majority. Nothing so cheers the duffer as to see a star look up or miss an easy shot. It brings balm to his own case of nervous upsets and many misses. For no man is safe from an attack of nerves in golf.

When Vardon and Ray tackled Ouimet at Brookline, there is no question but that both Englishmen were absolutely confident before the tournament started. Both expected him to crack early. When Ouimet refused to crack, it was a great study in golfing psychology to watch the two English stars. Both began to develop cases of nerves at the tenth hole, where each took three putts from within fair range of the cup. It was easy enough to imagine the range of their minds, and to imagine them saying: "What's this? Is it possible that we might be beaten by a youngster that no one in England ever heard of before? It isn't possible! It can't be done! He's bound to crack. But he seems to be getting better and better all the time. And if he doesn't crack he may beat us, after all!"

Ray was the first to crack, and the mighty Vardon followed him shortly afterward. In a nerve strain of that sort somebody had to crack, and since Ouimet didn't, the two great veterans did. This is a case that is hard to explain, for Vardon and Ray had the greater skill and the greater experience. But Ouimet on that occasion had such perfect control of his nerves that he was able to stand up where not even two masters could hold the pace.

NERVE VS. PHYSICAL MOULD

There are times when nerves are mixed up with physical inability to stand the grind of a tournament.

The most striking example of this involves the case of John Graham, the greatest amateur player in the world. Graham is the world's greatest amateur, despite the fact that he has never won a British Championship. It isn't a case of nerves with him, but as he is slight and not physically strong he simply is worn down physically before the week is over, and is a total wreck by the finish. In a thirty-six-hole medal-play competition he would be the favoured one over the field, as he has repeatedly won big tournaments of this sort. But under the strain of match play he is so badly worn down that he is unable to sleep. It is a queer fact that Graham, the best shot maker and the best medal player of England, and Evans, the best shot maker and best medal player in America, among amateurs, have neither been able to win an Amateur Championship. Evans has never been able to develop proper concentration—to get full control of his nerves in the amateur blue ribbon. Evans is extremely nervous, and this in spite of his rare skill. For an attack of nerves plays no favourites.

It may hit the best golfer in the world as quickly as it strikes the twelve handicap man.

If a star golfer, one who is experienced and a master of every shot in the bag, is unable to sleep the night before a tournament, and reaches the first tee haggard and nervous, how much more excuse is there for an average player, who takes his round just as seriously, but who knows that he hasn't the shots to back him up.

EXPLAIN THIS

Who can explain this situation? I have won four American Amateur Championships. I have been to the British Amateur twice, and have been eliminated both times in the first round. Evans is one of America's stars, but he has never got very far in England. Ouimet has won the Open and Amateur Championships of America, but was quickly put out in his English invasion. Yet Heinie Schmidt, not ranked among the first ten in the United States, goes over, and without any sign of a nervous upset, goes into the sixth round and is beaten only when Hilton, the champion, sinks a twenty-foot putt on the nineteenth hole. Schmidt showed more coolness and greater steadiness than any other amateur, except Travis, ever showed in the British premier. There was not a flutter to a nerve in his body. He played better golf than he knew how under the supreme test. Yet two months later, at Garden City, in the qualifying round for the United States Golf Amateur Championship, he failed even to qualify among the first thirty-two through nervously playing a short approach into a deep trap guarding the green.

All the psychologists in the world could never explain a temperamental shift of this sort. It is beyond the human understanding, and must simply take its place among the deep mysteries that surround the game.

INTO THE WHITE HEAT

Some time ago I was talking with one of the best golfers in the East. "Why is it," he asked, "that I can play such low-scoring rounds in friendly matches, and have so much trouble in big tournaments? Is it lack of nerve, or what?"

"Not at all," I said. "The answer is very simple. In your friendly rounds you never take your play with any great seriousness. You make no effort to concentrate. You play your shots naturally. There is nothing much at stake, and you have no curiosity that causes you to look up too quickly to see where the ball is going. This would be fine if you could maintain this same mental attitude in a big tournament. But no living man can. And so, not being used to long concentration, the strain is too great."

No golfer can jump from a series of carelessly played rounds into the white heat of a nerve-racking test and stand it as well as the golfer who has been training his mental attitude.

GOLF'S BIG FOUR

In golf four main ingredients are needed for tournament success: these are Skill, Temperament, Experience, and Luck. To allot each ingredient its percentage is a difficult task, but I would arrange the game's Big Four as follows: Skill, 50 per cent.; Temperament, 20 per cent.; Experience, 15 per cent.; Luck, 15 per cent.

We all know that skill is the ability to play the different shots, to drive, approach, and putt. We know what experience is, and we know what luck is.

But again—just what is this temperament? Here it is that the psychologists and experts and students of the game all sadly differ. Some call it courage; others call it lack of nerves; others call it control of nerves. But no satisfactory definition has ever been offered. The best definition I know is: Golf temperament is control of nerves, which is easily understood, plus the mental attitude for any one day, which is a mystery. It is this mental attitude for the day, this feeling that no man can tell on what day his game will be at its best or worst that causes all the trouble.

Here is an example of the latter section of temperament; i.e., mental attitude for the day. In the recent British Amateur Championship Harold Hilton had his hardest work cut out in the early part of the draw. Hilton, playing fine golf, won these early matches, and when he had defeated Harris it seemed that nothing could head him off from another championship. There was no golfer left supposed to be in his class. He should have had the feeling of utmost confidence. Then he met Blackwell. In this match Blackwell was not playing any wonderful golf. But on the first green Hilton took three putts. And from that point on his putting and his short game simply got beyond his grip. He fought his best, but could not get going. Why? There was no answer. He had rested well the night before. He had been playing fine golf. He had no feeling of nervousness at the start. He was confident of winning, and yet not unduly overconfident, knowing that Blackwell was an experienced golfer. Blackwell offered no brilliant golf to bring on any dismay. And yet the best part of Hilton's game was suddenly wrecked.

THE WINNING SHOT

No. Mr. Smith, duffer, has no reason to be depressed because his nerves are out of gear upon important occasions. If he expected to play a ninety, and returned a one hundred and four, it was through no cowardice or lack of nerve.

In 1911 Hilton made his first visit to America, where the odds were all against him, and with fine control of nerve won the championship from a big field.

In 1912 he came back, when the championship was held at Wheaton, Illinois. Here the odds were in his favour, for he had already made good and had experienced an American invasion the year before. But this time he was beaten in his first thirty-six-hole match by an almost unknown player in the ranking field, and largely because his game had suddenly got away from him on that day. It was not because he had not been playing well, because on the day before he had tied for the low score with Chick Evans in the qualifying round.

THE CASE OF McDERMOTT

Or, again, take the case of Jack McDermott, former American champion. Here was a golfer of rare skill, supreme confidence, and the soundest sort of nerve control. No one had ever been able to see a quiver in his golfing frame. Apparently his temperament was as wooden as the heart of an oak. He went to England and entered the British Open, and as America's greatest player he was expected to be well up with the field. He had played a practice round in seventy-one the day before when the preliminary round was started, what was Mc-Dermott's score? Seventy-one? Seventy-six? Or, say, ten strokes worse for an eighty-one? Not exactly! He returned a ninety-six, after one of the most wretched rounds of golf ever played in a big test. He had no control over any part of his game. No shot went right. And yet here was a golfer of wonderful temperament for match or medal play, and one possessing the rarest sort of skill and a fine backing of tournament experience. When Vardon came over two years ago he was paired with McDermott in a medal-play round at Shawnee, and the young American played with amazing nerve and confidence, and led his great English rival by thirteen strokes at the end of the seventy-two-hole test. Yet in the other test he had failed miserably.

BY WAY OF ENCOURAGEMENT

These examples of illustrious failures in the way of nerve control are not offered in any way as criticism upon those mentioned, but simply for the encouragement of those who have become discouraged or depressed through great nervousness under fire. No one can tell the amount of actual mental suffering that develops in every golf tournament. And a good part of this is due to the fact that each player has a certain feeling of shame in his fall-down, believing that outsiders will charge his lack of nerve control to cowardice. He feels that he is being branded as a quitter, and this helps spoil a big part of the pleasure to be derived from the game.

In a certain tournament one prominent golfer was entered who had made a reputation as a great football player, and largely through his nerve and dash. There could be no question about the quality of his heart. In this tournament he was drawn against an opponent that he should have beaten, but who soon settled down to some steady golf. The football player then, on at least five greens, missed short putts of less than three feet. It was pitiful, for any one could see that his nerves were jumping in a dozen different directions. There was positive agony on his face, as he felt, after missing each putt, that he was being charged right and left by the gallery with having a yellow streak.

Finally, when he had missed his fifth short putt, he could stand it no longer. Turning suddenly to the crowd he astonished the gallery by yelling out: "If any man here thinks I have a yellow streak, let him step out and I'll whip him with one hand." He knew in his heart that he wasn't a quitter, and yet for some inexplicable reason the evidence was so strong against him that he felt something must be done to prove his case. Every man who has played golf has had that great fear of being charged with cowardice or lack of nerve, because under certain tests his nervousness was so apparent that his game had gone to seed.

The average player, of course, suffers more than any one else, as he hasn't the skill to fall back on, or the experience that will sometimes check a rush of nerves to the surface. But if he will only stop and remember that at some time or another every player in the game has lost his nerve control, that great stars with skill and experience to back them up have all broken badly at various occasions and have played like novices, there should be no reason for his discouragement. Surely if a Vardon, a Ray, a Ouimet, or an Evans can fall down under pressure here and there, Mr. William Smith, duffer, should not be over-depressed because he tops a mashie shot or misses a short putt in some match that had jolted his nervous system out of fear. For in the broader sense it is not a question of courage, but merely of nerve control and the mysterious mental attitude that for one day may take any turn, and without offering the slightest warning as to which turn it will take.

THE ANCIENT AND ROYAL

A far green trail and a wide blue sky,

A clean white pill on a velvet lie;

And then—for a cut shot dead to the pin

And the thrill of a "three" as the putt drops in;

As it goes "klupp-klupp"—

In the old tin cup

And the score card shows that you stand two up—

Two up and the old home in sight—

Some game?   You said it—some game is right.

But to-morrow comes with a sudden switch

Where you miss your drive and you flub your pitch;

Where you thump to the trap with a maudlin curse

And your fourth shot out is a darned sight worse;

THE ANCIENT AND ROYAL

When you slice and top—
When you schlaff and flop—
When you hit the cup and the pill won't drop—
When you stand six down with your soul aflame—
Who said this smear was a regular game?

THE DUFFER TO THE PRO

You've handed me the proper form,
The proper stance and grip;
You've shown me how to swing the wood
And give the ball a flip;
You've shown me how to hold my head
And get the Follow Through—
Now show me how to get around
In Ninety One or *Two.*

You've shown me how H. Vardon swings
The driver from the tee;
You've shown me how the shoulder works
And eke the hip and knee;
You've shown me how each club is used—
To this, sir, I confess;
Now show me how to play around
In Ninety-Six—or less.

XII

GOLF VS. BUSINESS

IT IS generally understood that while a camel may plunge coyly through the eye of a needle, the assignment is by no means utterly devoid of complexity and a certain percentage of failure.

But the needle task allotted to the camel is absurdly simple compared to the job which confronts the golf-playing business man in attempting to live a double life.

A man involved in business—at least a business that absorbs a certain amount of time, labour, and worry—may play a very good game of golf—on occasions a very brilliant one—but it is only at rare intervals that he can carry the banner over championship ramparts and range himself with the really elect.

Golf helps business immensely, in that it furnishes

recreation and health for the tired business man. But this doesn't at all mean that business helps golf!

Golf is a matter of two main essentials—form and concentration. The golfer, neck high in some intricate business, may maintain perfect form to the last flick of his club. But when one's mental attitude has been punctured, harassed, pummelled, thwarted, cross cut, scrambled, and detached, by a variety of business troubles, it belongs only to the superman to rearrange and readjust the aforesaid mental attitude and focus it perfectly upon the task of playing a mashie over innumerable traps and bunkers to a small green surface 145 yards away. The business golfer may imagine that he has driven business cares and worries out of his brain, but subconsciously they are still a nagging force, diverting the eye from the ball or introducing a certain nervous tremor at exactly the wrong moment.

This idea is not only true, but it should have a soothing effect upon the multitudes simultaneously engaged in business and golf. For it certainly is a wonderful alibi, which is the most precious possession a golfer can have.

This last year a four times amateur champion decided to give most of his time to business as a member of the New York Stock Exchange. Those who knew golf said at once: "Good-bye to any more championships."

He felt exactly the same way.

"To win a championship," he said, "a man must give practically all of his time to golf through the playing season. As a side line it is still a fine thing, but no man can operate a side line into a championship. It isn't being done."

But in this one instance he was wrong, as he proved himself later on. When H. Chandler Egan, the great western golfer, won two amateur titles, he was giving most of his time to golf. Later he entered business and dropped from the very top rank.

Albert Seckel, the Princeton golfer who won the western amateur title one season and gave promise of being a permanent star, entered business soon after leaving college, and his name is heard no more.

Take again the case of Oswald Kirkby, Metropolitan and Jersey champion. In the spring—for two years—he has been able to devote a large amount of time to golf. In this way he has attached both the Metropolitan and Jersey Championships. But after May he has been forced to give up most of his time to business, with the result that while he is a very fine golfer, he has not been able to make any sort of showing in the Amateur Championships. We know of one prominent New York golfer, who in a fairly light and congenial business, played steadily in figures around 78 to 81. Later on he engaged in a business that was more nerve racking, and his scores immediately settled around 95.

Nearly all golf championships are won by those who give their entire time to golf. When Travers was winning championships golf was the major part of his spring and summer life. Walter J. Travis, who has won the amateur title on three occasions,

[254]

is editor of a golf magazine and gives most of his time to the game during every month in the year.

Francis Ouimet is connected, in a business way, with a sporting-goods house, and golf is a big part of his life.

"Chick" Evans, the great western player, is in the bond business, but he also writes golf for a daily paper, helps edit a golf magazine, and gives a big portion of his time to the game.

The two most eminent British amateurs of recent years are Harold Hilton and John Ball, who between them have won twelve championships. Hilton is editor of a golf magazine, and Ball conducts a hotel by the side of a golf course. For both of these men golf has been the main business of their careers.

The professional plays fine golf because golf is his very existence. He has nothing else to do—or think about. Jack McDermott, twice American Open Champion, attempted to engage in an outside business venture and his game went to pieces within a few months.

Golf is more a matter of concentration or co·ordination of mental faculties than anything else— that and eternal practice. It is a matter of rhythm and proper timing of stroke, details that develop from coördination of mind and muscle. So, when Business raises its scarred and seamy head between the golfer and his game, it acts as a perfect stymie.

The business man who tops his drive and flubs his approach can at least take consolation in the knowledge that he has fallen with the greatest stars of the game—champions until they exchanged the cleek for the fountain pen, or the brassie for the mahogany desk.

Too often the business man can't understand this situation. He can't understand why certain lapses should beset his game and deprive him of steadiness. But this is because concentration for him is often an effort, whereas for such golfers as Ouimet and Travis and Hilton and Ball and others, concentration on golf is a matter of course—a habit of long standing. These are not forced to make any effort to concentrate—as concentration upon each shot takes good care of itself the greater part of the time where these veterans are concerned.

A FREQUENT MISTAKE

These unnumbered golfers engrossed in business cares and worries and entangled in the art of making a living would find a quick improvement to their general play if they practised the system of less deliberation. If you will notice the majority of these around almost any golf course, you will see how unnecessarily slow most of them are.

This doesn't mean that a golf shot should ever be hurried or rushed. But neither should the golfer take so much time over the ball that he becomes rigid and taut, with all elasticity gone. There is nothing to be gained by standing like a statue until every muscle in the body has become like a piece of wood, and an early lack of confidence settles into a deadly conviction that shot is going wrong.

The business man, especially, should make it a

point to play along at a steady, even clip, and waste no more time than is necessary in getting the ball away. He will find that this method makes the matter of concentration much simpler. And of all who play, the business or professional man, with nerves close to the surface, can least afford to let his temper take control after a bad shot. For if nerves that have been at a quiver part of the day are not held in check during recreation, it is easy enough to see what a wreck there will be, not only of one's game —but of one's enjoyment and pleasure.

THE END

CPSIA information can be obtained
at www.ICGtesting.com
Printed in the USA
LVOW10s0924260717
542662LV00030B/1350/P